Success

Success Strategies

The Top 100 Best Ways To Be Successful

By Ace McCloud
Copyright © 2015

Disclaimer

The information provided in this book is designed to provide helpful information on the subjects discussed. This book is not meant to be used, nor should it be used, to diagnose or treat any medical condition. For diagnosis or treatment of any medical problem, consult your own physician. The publisher and author are not responsible for any specific health or allergy needs that may require medical supervision and are not liable for any damages or negative consequences from any treatment, action, application or preparation, to any person reading or following the information in this book. Any references included are provided for informational purposes only. Readers should be aware that any websites or links listed in this book may change.

Table of Contents

Introduction 6
Chapter 1: Success and Your Mental Wellbeing 8
Chapter 2: The Top 20 Habits of Peak Performers 21
Chapter 3: Health and Success 25
Chapter 4: Productivity and Self-Discipline 33
Chapter 5: Conquer Fear and Be Confident! 45
Chapter 6: Leadership and Team-Building 51
Chapter 7: Creativity, Organization and Success 61
Chapter 8: Finances and Success 66
Chapter 9: Ultimate Success Strategies 70
Chapter 10: Inspirational Quotes 77
Chapter 11: Your Personal Success Strategy 81
Conclusion 85
My Other Books and Audio Books 86

Be sure to check out my website for all my Books and Audio books.

www.AcesEbooks.com

Introduction

I want to thank you and congratulate you for buying the book, "Success: Success Strategies, The Top 100 Ways to be Successful."

Success is something that everybody seeks in life. Although the technical definition of success is "the accomplishment of an aim or purpose," many people internally create their own definitions. For some, success may mean finding happiness through material possessions, such as a car, a house, or another large asset. Other people tend to view success as working hard at their job and reaching the top. Many view it as having achieved financial tranquility, creating a family, falling in love, getting into shape, etc. As you can probably tell, everyone's personal definition of success is unique. Generally speaking, it is best to define success as something that brings personal satisfaction to you.

There are several core principles that I believe make up success: mental wellbeing, good habits, physical health, productivity, self-discipline, confidence, overcoming fear, leadership, creativity, organization and finances. More often than not, personal satisfaction lies within one or more of these areas. Think about somebody you know whom you regard as successful. He or she probably practices good habits, eats healthy and stays active and is relatively productive. Can you identify any other core success principles in that person? The answer, more than likely, is yes.

To achieve success is a great feeling. Most successful people are genuinely happy and have a positive outlook on life. Mastering most of the core success principles can help you feel great about yourself overall. While everybody has their own unique definition of success, I believe that being able to master each core principle can help you achieve an ultimate feeling of success. This book contains proven steps and strategies on how to master each core success principle as well as how to design a personal success plan to help you get there.

Within this book, you will discover how to strengthen your mental wellbeing, the top 20 habits of peak performing people, how to maintain your health and how to maximize your productivity for ultimate success. You will also discover how to practice self-discipline, boost your confidence, conquer your fears, be a leader and be creative. Finally, you will discover how to keep your life organized as well as manage your finances to become the most successful person you can be. As an added bonus, you will also find an entire chapter of inspirational and motivational quotes on success as well as the steps it takes to create your own customized success plan.

Chapter 1: Success and Your Mental Wellbeing

This chapter is all about how you can strengthen your mental wellbeing to work your way toward ultimate success. You will discover the benefits of creating and implementing a morning ritual into your life as well as how to set goals, eliminate negativity and excuses and practice forgiveness. Having a strong mental wellbeing is the first step to finding your personal satisfaction. Let's get started with the most important step...

Have a Morning Ritual

Many people find their lives are enhanced by performing a morning and/or evening ritual. It's a great way to start off and end your day, knowing exactly what you're going to do. A ritual is a certain succession of actions that help reinforce beliefs and attitudes.

What kind of attitude would you foster if every morning you woke up, turned off the alarm and grumbled when you had to get up? Surprisingly, or maybe not so surprisingly, this is what most people do. They would rather dream the day away in bed than meet it head long in order to reach and touch their dreams. How much better would their day go if they woke up with a smile ready to take on whatever came?

Rituals do not have to take much time. Waking up fifteen to twenty minutes early is all you really need, unless you want to incorporate physical exercise, a shower and getting ready. I personally started doing my new morning routine several months ago and I have noticed a huge difference in not only my productivity, but my overall energy level and happiness as well! To go along with that, my attitude has been great!

Check out the following suggestions on how to foster a positive attitude with a **morning ritual**:

1. As soon as consciousness seeps in; smile. Stretch those lips in an upward position to start your day off right.

2. Breathe deeply. This will get your blood circulating and start pumping blood through those muscles that have been relaxed and dormant all night long. Lie on your back and place your hands on your stomach under your ribs. Breathe in slowly and deliberately, preferably through your nose. As you breathe in, your stomach should puff out a bit. Your shoulders should not rise. Hold the breath and breathe out through your lips like you are blowing out a candle. Do this as slowly as you can. While you breathe out, your stomach near your ribs should suck in again. Take about five good breaths, thinking only about breathing in and out.

3. Once breathing is achieved, think of three or four things you are most grateful for. You may call to mind your family, your job, your pet or anything else. This should only take a few moments.

4. Breathe in and out quickly about ten times. This should clear your head and get you ready to start moving.

5. Stretch your muscles, starting at your neck and moving down to your shoulders, arms, hands, back and chest, your hips, stomach, thighs, legs and feet. If you need to sit up for this exercise, do so. Once you get good at it you will want to use the time while you stretch to think of a single goal or several that you wish to achieve. Then, set everything aside and get out of bed to take care of your needs.

6. First, go to the kitchen and drink a full glass of water. You can then exercise if you wish or start the shower. The water will get your digestive system ready to meet the day.

7. While in the shower, start your litany of positive affirmations. These are phrases that accomplish a goal or just make you feel good. Repeating positive affirmations is a method of self-hypnosis. If you keep saying it, you are affirming its truth and you will eventually believe it.

You can also affirm your goals during the affirmation stage of the morning ritual. For example, I affirm being a successful writer who can live off the money I make from writing. A business person might affirm becoming president of their company in five years. A teacher may affirm that he or she would reach the students in class so that they learn and are successful. Take a few more breaths and go out there to meet the day with a smile on your face and a bounce in your step.

Bonus Ideas For Morning Ritual

1. Don't check your email within thirty minutes of waking up in the morning! If you ignore your email and do your morning ritual first, statistics show that you are over 30% more likely to be more productive during that day.

2. Read for fifteen minutes from a self-development or similarly uplifting source of information.

3. Listen to favorite music while stretching or doing yoga for twenty minutes or so.

4. Review all of your goals and then visualize yourself completing them as you feel the emotions that go along with their accomplishment! Make a strategic plan that has you doing the most important things first in the day and finishing everything else after that.

5. Eat a nutritious meal early in the day. One of my favorites is organic baby spinach and a banana mixed in my Nutribullet blender to make a delicious and energizing smoothie.

Your **evening ritual**, should you choose to do it, should focus on calming the body and mind in order to ready it for sleep, while still fostering a positive attitude. Here are a few steps you can follow to perform an evening ritual:

1. Do some deep breathing. Deep breathing does waken the body, but it also induces relaxation. Lie in the bed and slowly breathe in and out, as you did in the morning. Do this five to six times concentrating only on the breaths you are taking. Empty the mind of everything else.

2. As you set your alarm, think about your day. Evaluate progress toward your goals and think of three things you did that fulfilled your morning affirmations.

3. If you pray, say your evening prayers. If you do not pray, reinforce some of your favorite affirmations.

4. Have a good night's sleep.

Goals and Goal-Setting

Without setting a goal, you are very likely to never achieve success. Your goals serve as the roadmap that keeps you on track. Without goals, you are more likely to wander in any direction and less likely to achieve things of lasting value. This section is all about goal-setting and what you can do to ensure you're doing it right.

Develop Your Goals and Action Plan. To be motivated for anything, it is essential to set goals and know what you're going to do to reach them. Without goals, it is very hard to intelligently make a plan to steer your life in the direction desired. The first thing you can do to stay motivated in your life is to set goals and review them several times per day. A good and effective idea is to write your ideas down on paper and put them in a place where you can easily review them. When you write something down, you tend to retain it much better. Take a few minutes and write down some goals, if you don't have them already. A good strategy to utilize when making a goal is to make it seem easy. For example: I will easily workout four times per week, or I will easily increase my income by two thousand dollars a month by the end of the year. Be sure to be very specific about your goals and why you want to achieve them. Make this vision compelling and something that really excites you. Too many people make small goals that lack passion; don't be afraid to dream big and shoot for something truly incredible. Once you know what your goals are, the next thing is to develop an action plan.

Having goals is great but if you don't know how to work towards them, you will more than likely never reach them. Let's say that one of your goals is to start saving more money. You've got your goal—now think about your action plan. One idea could be to state that you will put aside some extra money each week into a special bank account. Another idea would be to list all of your expenses, and then to strategically go through them to see which ones can be reduced and which can be eliminated. Then plan to read your goals and action plans at least once a day, if not more, to help keep you focused and motivated towards accomplishing your goals. Any time you are feeling unmotivated to keep up on your finances, refer back to your goals and action plans.

Figure Out Why Your Goals Matter. If you are not sure why you set the goals that you set for yourself, you may not feel as motivated to work toward them. By asking yourself *why* you want to reach each goal, you can be reminded of its true purpose.

The power of asking the question "why" can hugely help you achieve success. Many people do not need a tangible award to find satisfaction. Often, they are inspired to do something just for the enjoyment it brings to them or others. For example, if you asked yourself, "*Why* do I work out hard?" your answer may be, "Because I want to look great in my bathing suit." Why do you work two jobs? "Because I love my kids and want to give them the best life possible." Whenever you ask yourself why you want to do something, it should be followed with an answer that starts with, "Because..."

Asking the question "Why?" can be a very powerful success strategy in almost every aspect of your life and career. When you were a young child, you probably asked your parents, "Why?" many times. It was because you wanted to better understand how things worked. However, learning is never-ending, and even as an adult, you can still use the question "Why?" to gain a deeper understanding of how things work. By gaining a deeper understanding of how things work, your chances of feeling more inspired to move towards your goals will likely be much higher.

Asking the question "Why?" is how many people end up making changes in themselves and in the world. This is usually because asking "Why?" can lead you to the root cause of a problem. When you know the root cause of a problem, you can work on fixing it. I know this can sound a little confusing, so I will use a specific example to try and make this a bit clearer.

Let's say that you had a great idea...a solution to a worldwide problem. It could help people for years. However, to get that idea out to the world, you would have to put yourself out there and push it. While this may not be hard for some people, it could be much more difficult if you have a strong fear of failure or if you dread speaking in public. So, if you were to allow your fear of public speaking to overcome you, then it is likely your idea wouldn't make it very far and few lives would be changed. By simply asking yourself, "Why am I fearful of public speaking?" you can figure out the root cause. You may have suffered a bad experience when you were younger.

Common negative experiences in public speaking include getting teased by classmates or getting reprimanded by your teacher while you spoke in front of everybody.

Once you've figured out the root cause of your fear of public speaking, you will then be more aware why it exists and, consequently be able to take steps to fix it. You can work to improve your public speaking skills and self-confidence until you're ready to face large audiences. Now, if you hadn't asked yourself, "Why am I fearful of public speaking?" you may have never been able to overcome your fear and get your great ideas out to the world. Do you now have a better understanding of the power of asking "why?"

When thinking about your past, ask yourself why you felt a certain way and then learn from that experience. When making a decision in the present moment, ask yourself why you would pick one route over the other. By taking a few moments to ask yourself this one word question, you can master a very powerful, yet simple, tool. Once you have the answer, be sure to write it down and remind yourself of it often. Use it as fuel to keep you inspired and keep you moving towards your goal.

So, any time you feel tempted to spend that extra $20 that you could be saving, think about *why* your goals matter. More than likely, this will help you stay motivated. One good idea to help yourself figure out why your goals matter is to write each one down and then write your thoughts on why you want to achieve them. You can use that opportunity to brainstorm your thoughts. You may end up coming up with several great reasons for each goal, which can push you even further to pursue your dreams.

- **Bonus: Don't Think About Materialism.** Throughout life, it can be easy to get caught up in the world of commercialism or materialism—that is, focusing more on what physical things you can get (money, clothes, jewelry, cars, the latest electronics, etc.). Get into the mindset that it is better to give and live in the present moment, rather than to try and get all the assets you can. By getting into this habit, you can see just how great life can be without having the latest popular sneakers or the latest handbag. You can focus more on finding ways to tackle real-life issues for both yourself and others. A great strategy for doing this is to brainstorm the things in your life that you can give thanks for. You may be surprised at just how prosperous you truly are. This may free you to spend your precious mental energies on truly important matters instead of being envious, jealous, or always wanting more.

Focus on Values, Be Successful. Get into the habit of focusing on your core values. Some of the most common values that people hold dear are their families, their religion, and their morals. Most of the time, your values are enough to inspire you to accomplish great things. For example, you might be inspired to start your own business because your parents struggled with hourly jobs and you do not want to provide that kind of life for your family. As long as your actions reflect your values, your chances of success will be greater.

Practice Accountability. By setting goals in the first place, you are greatly increasing your chances of achieving them. Some of your goals, especially your personal goals, may be private, meaning that only you know about them. To stay motivated to achieve them, you can practice accountability to reach your end result.

Practicing accountability is easy to do. If you don't mind other people knowing about your goals, you could hold yourself accountable on social media. If you prefer your goals to stay private, you could ask a close friend, a relative, or your partner to help you stay accountable. Many people call this an accountability partner. Set up plans for your accountability buddy to contact you once a week and ask how your goals are. By having somebody else hold you accountable, your chances of sticking to your goals can be higher.

For example, if you're trying to save money, ask somebody to call you up once a week and ask, "So how much have you saved so far?" If the answer doesn't meet the required goal, then there could institute some sort of penalty for failure. This penalty should keep you motivated to get things done the right way during the week.

- **Bonus: Find Your Accountability Partner!** When you are alone in an endeavor, it tends to be much harder to accomplish things. If your friends, family, and loved ones do not agree with your goals, their chances of discouraging you tend to be much higher. However, even if your family and friends don't support you, you can still overcome this obstacle. Whenever you have the chance, take some time and connect with like-minded people. For example, if you're a writer trying to make it big, go online and find others with a similar goal. By building up your network of support, you can feel much more motivated. Also, when you stick to your efforts, you can experience great personal fulfillment. Remember, whatever you are doing is for yourself, not for anybody else. Don't forget to be your own support! Some of the greatest things in history have been accomplished by people who ignored their friends, family, teachers, and everyone else to follow their passion and make their dreams a reality.

- **Bonus: Be Reliable and Trustworthy.** Live up to your commitments and go through with the things you promise. This can help you stay on top of your game, whether at home or at work. For example, if you say you're going to start a fundraiser, do it; go through with it. When you take immediate action, you are more likely to complete your task; by so doing you strengthen your ability to keep your word in the future. Doing this also helps you become more credible and reliable to others — and that can often open up even more opportunities. People who can be relied upon and trusted are greatly revered in society, but those who get through life by lying, making excuses, and performing poorly are generally looked down upon and disliked.

Overcome Future Obstacles Now. As with any goal, you will usually run into an obstacle or two along the way. For example, if you're trying to stick to a diet and you go to a Christmas party, your obstacle will probably be all of the delicious-looking foods and desserts that people bring. If your goal is to get a promotion at work, an obstacle might be that you will have to get extra work done in less time or outperform an ambitious colleague. By thinking about what your future obstacles may be, you can strategize solutions to these problems before they even occur. It is much better to be prepared than to realize one day after many hours of work that you didn't anticipate a critical detail that is going to set you behind dramatically. Take your time to be smart, do your research, and the majority of the time you will come out smelling like a rose.

Of course, you may run into an obstacle that you couldn't predict—if that happens, just stay positive and work through it. Maybe you are trying to save money but then your car engine fails. Unfortunately, you probably couldn't foresee that, especially if you have a newer car. Don't be discouraged. One good thing about obstacles is that they make you stronger. By trying to predict some of the more common obstacles associated with your goals, you will be less likely to get discouraged in the event of a roadblock.

Prepare For Failure. This technique is a little similar to the technique about trying to predict your obstacles but it does have some unique aspects. As you probably know, sometimes you will not win. Sometimes you will not reach your goal or you won't reach it in the time frame that you wanted. To stop yourself from becoming discouraged, prepare for failure.

Prep yourself to look at failure in a positive light. If you try something and you fail, you may realize that you need to do something differently. Don't view it as a complete loss—view it as a lesson learned. Tell yourself that you will not make the same mistake in your next venture. If you start working toward a huge goal with high expectations, just to find out that you won't be able to make it, you will most likely become very disappointed. While you shouldn't *not* reach for the stars, just make a conscious choice to use failure to your advantage if it does occur. Sometimes more important things pop up or life gets in the way. As you have already heard many times before, one of the great keys to success is just to never give up. Keep moving forward with dogged determination, despite any setbacks that may occur along the way and eventually you will get there.

View Your Most Important Tasks From a Different Angle. When it comes to reaching your goals, sometimes you have to prioritize your most important tasks to stay motivated—otherwise, you can get caught up in things that don't matter. Sometimes, your most important tasks in reaching your goals can seem hard, boring, and annoying. Instead of looking at those tasks as "musts," look at them as "wants."

By doing your most important tasks first, you can get closer to what you want. Looking at your goals in this way is a great technique for staying motivated. Also, a great way to prioritize your most important tasks is to create a to-do list or keep a planner handy. When you're able to plan and organize your days, your chance of taking steps toward your goals gets better. When I am working at my desk, I like to cut up small pieces of white paper and put down on each one a goal that needs to be accomplished. I will then arrange those pieces of paper in order from the most important down and then throw away each paper when its task is complete.

- **Bonus: Appreciate Your Challenges.** Make it a habit to look at your challenges and struggles in a positive light—they brought you to where you are now. Anticipate your future challenges and struggles as things that will help you learn and grow. Whenever you're feeling discouraged, remind yourself of a previous challenge that you overcame and in what ways it positively affected your life—this can help you get through the next challenge.

Reward and Give Yourself Credit. While working to reach your goals, one great way to stay motivated is to reward and credit yourself for your progress. Rewards are a great incentive and motivator because who doesn't love getting rewarded? If you're working toward a long-term goal and you reward yourself for every step you take toward it, don't reward yourself with the same thing every time—switch it up and you will be less likely to get bored. You can reward yourself with a vacation, a nice dinner, a full body massage, a trip to the movies, or anything else that you find appropriate.

Give yourself credit, too. If your goal is to put on five pounds of muscle in three months, check the scale at the end of each month and say, "I knew I could do it! Now I am much stronger and I will only get better!"

- **Bonus: Avoid Impatience.** You shouldn't confuse being impatient with having a sense of urgency, but if you are impatient, you will not likely get very far in life and towards your goals. When you're impatient, you tend to forget things or make more mistakes than if you had slowed down and paid more attention. Sometimes impatience can be hard to tackle. It's different for everybody, but one really good technique is to take a lot of breaks. Breaks can help you slow down and refocus on whatever it is that you're working on. Another good idea to is think about the great results that you can end up with when you exert a little bit of patience. Being impatient can give you a very bad reputation if you are rushing through things, being sloppy, cutting corners, and delivering subpar results that could easily have been rectified by taking the time necessary to do the task properly.
- Bonus: Avoid Vagueness. If you are vague in your goals or your future plans, it can be hard to stay motivated. You need a clear picture of what you really want. To help keep your motivation alive, be specific in your goals, actions, and plans. Only clear-cut objectives will allow you to see possible steps to reach them. Visualizing your goals can help you feel what it will be like to achieve the end results.

Visualization

Visualization can be a very powerful technique for staying motivated and achieving success. It is something that the top pros in the world do on a consistent basis.

Think about what you want and why you want it. Then, imagine what your life will be like once you've got it. For example, if you are struggling financially, think about what your life will be like once you've saved money: you can relax knowing that you're a little more financially secure; you won't have to spend so much money on public transportation, because you'll have enough money to buy a car. Everything you visualize will be different, based upon your individual goals and your own needs. To dramatically increase your chances for success, I suggest you make visualization a daily habit. It is also a good idea to visualize a scene in the third person, as if you were observing it from ten to fifteen feet away. Just allow the scene to flow naturally, with you doing everything perfectly to achieve your desired goal.

Let's look at a famous example to see just how powerful and inspiring visualization can be. Jim Carrey, the actor, used to park his car in famous spots in California to feel what his life would be like when he made it big. He even wrote himself a huge check and dated it for five years in the future. Shortly after he dated that check, he was paid $10,000,000 to be act the movie *Dumb and Dumber*.

If visualization could inspire somebody like Jim Carrey to do great things in his life, imagine what it could help you do in *your* life! Still not convinced? Leave it to science—your brain is programmed in a way in which it cannot tell the difference between reality and a projected reality. That means that visualization is a proven technique for reaching your goals. Try this short technique to help you reach a powerful visualization:

My first suggestion is to **include all of your senses in your vision**. Imagine what you'll hear, imagine what you'll touch, and imagine what you'll taste. Even think about what you'll smell. Picture how you will celebrate your accomplishment, how you'll laugh, smile, and enjoy life. Really submerge yourself in your vision. Make it as real as possible.

The second thing is to **visualize your accomplishments from different angles**. See yourself as if you were in a movie and you are the lead role. Picture yourself reaching your dreams from your own eyes and then picture how others will see it. Picture it as if you were reading a book written about yourself in the third-person. Each time you visualize your success, choose a different set of eyes through which to picture your achievement.

The third step is to start to **live as if your goals and dreams are reality**. Dress the way you would dress if you were an entrepreneur and act as you would act if you were a doctor. Whatever you want to do, start living and acting like you already do it. Live your life so that you give off a vibe of who you eventually want to be.

The next thing is to **pair affirmations with your mental images**. Say things to yourself that you can imagine others saying about you once you've made it. Create your positive affirmations from different viewpoints, just as you did with your visualizations.

Finally, I highly suggest that you **make a visual representation** of your objective. One idea is to put together a collage of your dreams. You may wish to hang up inspirational quotes in your workspace. You could use pictures or put together a video. You can do anything that works for you, as long as it serves to remind you daily of where you are headed. For this to be successful, you need to look at your visual reminder daily, multiple times a day if possible. Just noticing it once a week or paying attention to it off and on will not be enough to make a noticeable difference.

Positive Affirmations

Positive thoughts can help you take action whenever you feel inspired and therefore may lead you to success. They also leave you in a better position to recognize and capitalize on good opportunities. If your head is filled with negative thoughts, your ability to be inspired and take action can severely decline. While it is definitely not always easy to do this, here are some good steps to take to get you thinking positively.

Positive affirmations are excellent for combatting negative thoughts. Come up with empowering phrases and repeat them over and over in your head. Over time, these positive phrases can override many of the negative thoughts that pop up in all of us from time to time. An example of a **good positive affirmation** is: "I am strong, happy, healthy, and loving life!" Another good idea is to limit your exposure to negative people. Try and surround yourself with positive and uplifting people and you may be surprised at how much happier and inspired you can be. Here are some great positive affirmations that you can start out with - Sooner than later you may find yourself coming up with your own:

- I deserve to be happy.

- I am smart enough and organized enough to be able to get a good paying job.

- I am worthy of love.

- I see the good in all people and situations.

- I love my life.

- I am generous, giving and caring every day of my life.

- I act quickly and decisively.

- I am going to be a winner today.

- I will improve myself every day by following good habits, eating healthy and promoting good relationships in my life.

- I am super strong, healthy, wealthy, and wise.//
- I am super creative and perform flawlessly.

Bonus: Avoid Jealousy. Jealousy is a huge motivational killer because when you get wrapped up in it, you tend to get caught up on how you *don't* have something instead of spending that time trying to get it for yourself. Most likely, you have friends who love to show things off in real life and on social media—sometimes seeing something on social media is the worst because you automatically think that someone else is living the perfect life while you're not. Any time you are feeling jealous, don't let yourself get wrapped up in it—instead, think about what kind of goals you can set to get the things going that *you* want, and start to work on them. By knowing that you will be working toward getting something that you really want, your chances of achieving it will be much higher.

Eliminate Negativity

Negativity is a horrible emotion that generally serves no good purpose. Negativity is often a huge factor in why people become unmotivated. When you constantly hear negative thoughts, it is much easier to become discouraged from whatever it is you want to do. Eliminate negative people from your life and start finding friends who have positive thoughts. Although this is a challenge, if you can do it, I promise you will instantly feel the improvements it can bring to your life. I can't tell you how many people in my life people have underestimated me, told me I couldn't do things, and actually tried to prevent me from reaching my dreams. This is common to most everyone, whether you are a pro or a regular person. The best strategy is to prove the losers wrong by using their criticism as motivation to reach your goals. It is extremely satisfying to see the look on other peoples' faces after you have just put on a peak performance that has dominated!

It is also a great idea to stay away from the newspapers and the news. It is extremely difficult to keep a positive frame of mind when you are filling your brain with all the horrible things that happened in the last day or week. I know you have probably heard this before... but actually do it! Try switching out the news for reading motivational and inspiring books. Over the long term, you may be shocked at what such a simple change can do in your everyday life!

Also, be sure to catch any negative thoughts that you might be sending to yourself. A great strategy for this is to write down your negative thoughts throughout the day. By writing them down and seeing them, you can have a better sense of how they are not true and how they will not help you. For example, if you think, "I'll never save any money," write that down and then tell yourself how it's not true. Another great strategy is to simply wear a rubber band on your wrist, and every time a negative thought pops in your head, snap it. This strategy has worked great for me and others I know as well.

A lot of times, negativity comes from fear. If you find yourself feeling anxious or afraid all of the time, it is critical that you eliminate this fear so that you can feel positive and uplifting emotions on a regular basis. There is nothing more damaging to motivation then constantly running fears through your mind all day long.

- **Bonus: Be Unique and Different.** A great poem once spoke of a person picking one of two paths to walk down. The person picked the path that was obviously not traveled by many people; later he went on to say that it was a great choice. Be like the person in that poem; be brave. Be courageous. Dare to be different and do things that other people typically wouldn't do (positive, legal things, of course!). Although you can sometimes feel like people look at you strangely when you're different, many people secretly admire your ability to be unique.

Eliminate Excuses

Excuses are a big reason many people fall into the groove of becoming unmotivated and unsuccessful. When you continually make excuses for why you are not progressing toward your goals, you will likely never achieve success. A good way to catch an excuse is when you hear yourself saying, "**But**." Whenever you hear or feel that word coming off your tongue, stop yourself and don't let it come out.

For example, if you hear yourself saying, "I really want to put this $20 away for the future *but* I also really want this new shirt..." immediately recognize that you're making an excuse for not sticking to your goal. Another good idea is to use reverse psychology on your excuses. For example, you could say, "I really want to buy that new shirt *but* if I do that, I won't reach my goal of saving."

- **Bonus: Avoid Being Ungrateful.** When you're ungrateful, it is easy to lose sight of the small things in life, which often become the most important things when they're suddenly taken away. Practicing gratitude can help you learn how to appreciate the things around you and in your life. Being grateful can help you stay motivated because it feels good, you know what your values are, and you can gain a better sense of your hard work. When you are halfway to reaching one of your goals, be grateful that you got that far and be grateful for what you've learned in the process. That way, you will want to go on and get the end results. Also, be sure to be grateful for all the other incredible things in your life.

Take Risks. Unless you take risks in your life, you may miss out on some of the best opportunities. In other words, you don't know if you will succeed at something unless you try. That way, if you do fail, you will know that you gave it your all and you will have a better chance at feeling inspired to try something else. Want to help the less fortunate? Do it! Want to apply for your dream job? Do it! Never give up! Many times in life, the most successful people aren't the smartest or the most qualified; they are the ones brave enough to take a risk and go for their dreams.

Forgiveness and Keeping the Past in the Past

If you focus too much on your past instead of your present, the chances of creating a better future for yourself may decrease dramatically. If you allow your past to remain constantly before you, you will find yourself circling it endlessly, unable to break free to pursue the future. Your present choices can seriously affect your future. If you must focus on the past, use it to inspire yourself to grow, improve, and change.

Utilize the **healing power of forgiveness** to put the past in its proper place. We all experience anger, resentment, hatred, and other unhealthy emotions. These contribute nothing towards our real life. By allowing yourself to forgive the people and circumstances in the past that stir up these emotions, you can instead focus on more positive and uplifting realities that can help you move forward in your life.

Chapter 2: The Top 20 Habits of Peak Performers

Practicing good habits is essential to becoming successful. Habits are actions that you repeat so frequently that they become automatically programmed in your brain. Habits can be good or bad. Most peak performers practice beneficial habits, many of which you will learn about in this chapter.

1. **Learn to Handle Rejection.** Rejection is inevitable. At one point or another in your life, you will probably be turned down—whether you're rejected from a sports team, a college, a position or something else. Many people tend to let a rejection discourage them, but if you can learn to view rejection in a positive light, you can better position yourself to succeed when the next opportunity arises. If you are rejected, see it as a chance to learn what you can improve upon. Don't get all emotional if someone gives you criticism. They are usually just trying to help. If you can learn to receive criticism without blowing your lid, then you will be much better off in your journey through life.

2. **Be Yourself.** Believe it or not, many people get so caught up in trying to be like other people that they forget to be themselves. If you try to impress a person by dressing differently from your true style, you aren't being yourself. Bending your opinion to agree with someone else is another example. When you are yourself in the way that you dress, think, talk, and act, it is usually much easier to be happy and relaxed. Most people are quite adept at knowing when you are being a fake; they find it quite a turn off. Since most deceptions are eventually uncovered, it is best to just be yourself in the first place.

3. **Learn From Your Mistakes.** You can't learn unless you make mistakes. Many people allow their mistakes to discourage them but if you can view them as learning experiences, you will always gain personal growth. The key is to learn from your mistake the first time. For example, if you neglect to brush your teeth and have to spend thousands of dollars on dental work, you should learn from that to take better care of your teeth so it doesn't happen again. Even better than learning from your mistakes is to seek the advice of a mentor or read a good book on the subject you're currently interested in. Preventing mistakes by taking the advice of others is the best route to take.

4. **Keep Your Workspace Clean and Organized.** If your workspace is cluttered or messy, your productivity levels can drastically decline. Important papers, ideas, or tasks can get swallowed in the clutter. A cluttered desk can also cause mental stress. It is important to get into the habit of keeping a clean and organized workspace. You can get into this habit by using desk organizing tools (like a paper holder or pen holder), organizational computer programs, and train yourself to throw away any food or drinks that you consume at your desk as soon as you're finished with them. You may be

surprised at how much better you feel when you have a crisp and clean workplace free from clutter and distractions. More on this topic in a few chapters.

5. **Ask For Help.** Asking others for help when you need it is a great habit. We can easily get caught up in too much pride and be afraid to ask others for help when we truly need it. For example, some people can be stubborn and refuse to let anyone help them lift a couch. Others may be embarrassed to ask for help with a project out of fear that it will make them look stupid. The truth is, asking for help will not make you look stupid or weak. Besides, people are often more than happy to help; but they don't need help if you don't ask. If you do not learn how to ask for help, you risk having your workload pile up to add even more stress in your life. If it comes to something like asking for help to lift something heavy, you may run the risk of hurting yourself. Being helpful is human nature, so if you tend to try and do everything by yourself, you may want to try making this more of a habit.

6. **To-Do Lists.** To-do lists may seem like a silly thing to do, but they can actually help you manage your day much more effectively. By getting into the habit of writing a to-do list each morning, you can have a better idea of how your day will flow. It can also help you organize and prioritize your tasks, which can help improve your productivity tremendously.

7. **Make Time for Breakfast.** Out of all the meals you have in a day, breakfast is the most important. It is the first thing that you put in your body each morning, which can make all the difference in terms of your energy. If you do not eat breakfast and you dive straight into your day, your chances of feeling tired, weak, and sluggish by the afternoon can greatly increase. When you do get into the habit of eating breakfast, make sure it's a healthy one!

8. **Sleep Right.** Getting into good sleeping habits can have tremendous benefits on both your physical *and* your mental health. Your body can suffer many consequences without the proper amounts of sleep. A lack of sleep can cause you to become lazy and unproductive, which will only lead you in the opposite direction from success. The most effective sleeping habit is to have a consistent sleeping schedule. By going to bed and waking up at the same time, your body and biological clock have a better chance to regulate. Another good way to ensure that you can sleep well is to make sure you sleep in a dark area and on a comfortable bed.

9. **Exercise.** Exercising your body is one of the best habits ever. As you probably know, exercising is a great way to look and feel excellent. It can help increase your longevity and it can fend off stress. To get into the habit of exercising, you can start off small. For example, start by walking on the sidewalk and gradually work your way up to learning strength exercises. By getting into this habit, you can increase your chances of feeling energetic, productive, and motivated. Many of the world's top performers have exercise as one of their primary habits. More on exercise and health in a few chapters.

10. **Remember to Laugh.** Some people believe that the best type of medicine is laughter. Laughter is a well-known stress-relieving technique. Think about the last time you shared a funny moment with your family or exchanged a joke with a friend. Chances are that you felt happy and joyful in that moment. If you tend to be serious and uptight, you may sometimes forget to have a laugh and your stress levels could be higher than necessary. Remembering to laugh is an easy habit to get into. You can get your laughs in by downloading a jokes app to your phone, tuning into the Comedy Channel on your TV, buying a humorous book, or by spending time with others who love to laugh.

11. **Be Optimistic.** Have you ever heard that attitude is everything? People who have negative attitudes tend to be followed by negative actions and consequences. People who have optimistic and positive attitudes are more likely to realize their dreams and know success. By simply having a positive outlook on life, your chances of living a fulfilling life can increase. For example, say that your friend worked a high-paying job and you worked a minimum wage job. If you constantly mope and wallow over the fact that your friend makes more money than you, you will be too distracted to figure out how to improve your own paycheck. Studies have shown that optimistic people have a much higher chance of spotting opportunities and capitalizing on them than pessimistic people.

12. **Resist Fear.** Fear is a natural emotion, but many allow it to control their lives. It is normal to be afraid to take risks in your life but sometimes you can deny yourself a great opportunity if you don't chance it. As you know, learning how to resist fear can open many potential doors for your future. One great way to resist fear is to think about exactly what is holding you back, then focus on that specific fear. Even a thousand years ago people knew that fortune favors the brave. More details on overcoming fear will be provided in a few chapters.

13. **Prioritize Your Tasks.** By knowing which tasks on your to-do list are the most important, you can push the less important tasks to the end. When you take care of your most important tasks, you can work hard in the beginning and relax later.

14. **Follow the 80/20 Rule.** The 80/20 rule is a well-known theory that suggests a great way for people to stay productive. The idea is that if you focus on the most important 20% of a task that produces the best results and mostly ignore the other 80%, then you will end up getting much better results. For example, if you're a baker and you notice that the majority of your sales come from fresh donuts, then it would be wise to focus the majority of your attention on making fresh donuts rather on other items that aren't bringing in as much revenue. More on the 80/20 Rule in a few chapters.

15. **Practice S.M.A.R.T.** Before you try to tackle a bunch of tasks at once, ask yourself if each one is specific, measurable, attainable, relevant, and timely

(S.M.A.R.T). If the answer is "no," then you might want to put that task off until a later date. Getting into the habit of measuring your tasks with this acronym can save you a lot of time.

16. **Turn Off Social Media.** Social media, such as Facebook, Twitter, YouTube, and Google+, are great for networking and learning information, but they can also be very distracting. If you have access to the internet on your work computer, see if you can block yourself from accessing those websites. If you have social media apps on your phone, simply turn your phone off while you're working. You can always go back to social media during your free time or save it as your "reward" for achieving success.

17. **Don't Complain.** It can be tempting to complain about your job or your responsibilities, but nothing good ever came from complaining. It doesn't change your situation and if your boss or coworkers overhear you complaining about your job, it can tarnish your character and limit your chances for advancement. Complaining can also be mentally draining, so it is not even worth doing.

18. **Finish Anything You Start.** By finishing any projects that you start, you can show others you're a hard-working, dedicated, and committed person. Once you've finished what you've started, you can also feel good about yourself, knowing that you can accomplish things and follow through on the things that you say.

19. **Set Tomorrow Up, Tonight.** Setting up your next day on the night before can be an excellent habit. You could simply make a to-do list of everything that needs to be done, whether at work or at home. You could lay your clothes out the night before, set up your breakfast food for easy preparation, stretch, or do anything else that can help you to prepare for the next day. This can save you time and energy to get other things done.

20. **Set Goals.** As you discovered a few pages ago, setting goals is one of the most important habits you can develop to become a peak-performing person.

Chapter 3: Health and Success

Maintaining a healthy diet and keeping your body in overall good physical health is an important step to reaching success. This chapter is all about the steps you can take to establish a strong health routine, including how to create the ultimate diet plan and how to integrate physical exercise into that plan. You will also discover the benefits of using vitamins, minerals and supplements as well as the benefits of getting a good night's sleep. Many successful people also successfully take care of their bodies. Let's start with your diet:

Creating the Ultimate Diet Plan

To be able to efficiently manage your diet, I highly recommend having a **plan**. Creating a personalized diet plan can help you better address your eating preferences while working around your school or work schedule. It can also serve as a visual or a map, which can make your diet easier to follow.

The first thing you should do when creating a personalized diet plan is to reflect upon yourself. The better you know yourself, the better you can figure out what kind of diet plan you need in order to see successful results. There are a couple of basic, key questions that you can ask yourself to start out:

First, ask yourself **how many meals** you would like to eat per day. Some people can get away with eating two meals but others may like to break their meals up. I would highly recommend breaking your meals up into smaller portions and eating four to five times per day.

When you've figured out how many meals you want to eat per day, you can try to divide the total amount of calories you want to consume each day by the number of meals that you eat each day. For example, if you only want to eat two thousand calories per day, you can eat four meals of five hundred calories or two meals of one thousand calories, or any such combination. Here is one tip: you should try to eat at least three meals per day. Eating smaller meals consistently can help prevent overeating and increase overall alertness and energy level. If you are doing strength training and regular exercise, you often times do not even have to count calories, just eat healthy and when you're hungry. Over time this strategy tends to lead towards an athletic and strong body that is not overweight.

Secondly, ask yourself **how much time** you will be able to spend putting your meals together. If you're not a fan of cooking or if you have a busy schedule, you will have to figure out how you're going to coordinate your meal preparation. This will all depend on your own schedule. For example, it might be better for you to prepare all of your meals in advance on Sunday night and keep them in your refrigerator/freezer. This strategy can save you lots of time compared to preparing a fresh meal each night.

Thirdly, take a minute to **think about your relationships and support**. To be successful at anything, having a strong and encouraging support system can help you reach your goals. You can ask your family and friends if they would like to diet with you, which can help make the process easier. If they do not want to diet with you, ask them to be supportive of your decision. You might even want to find somebody else who is dieting, eating healthy, or interested in being a workout buddy to help keep you motivated.

Fourthly, if you know you're going to eat out at a restaurant, try to **find out what their menu is like** beforehand. Make sure you take into account everything that you eat and try to pick out the healthiest options. You can even stick to your diet when eating out by making simple swaps, such as getting fresh vegetables instead of fries or skipping out on the free bread.

Fifthly, **don't leave your sweet tooth** in the dust. Being on a diet does not mean that you can never have a treat again; it just means that you have to be more aware of what you're having and how much of it you're consuming. If you tend to crave junk food, make room for it in your diet so that you don't binge on it later. A good idea is to set aside 100 calories in your diet for when you're having a junk food craving. Chocolate is always a favorite, and dark chocolate is actually healthy for you. Just choose something that you like as a reward for all your hard work.

The best part about creating a personal diet plan is that you get to choose what kinds of foods you want to eat every day. As you begin to create your own diet plan, think about the different kinds of foods you can include from each food group. When planning out your meals, take these few tips into consideration:

- You can stay full by combining protein and fiber. Your body will feel more satisfied by having a lunch that consists of a piece of fruit, a yogurt cup, and a cooked egg rather than a bag of chips and a soda. A really great, easy lunch that has worked out for me is combining four tablespoons of low-fat, vanilla yogurt with a bowl of pumpkin flavored granola. It keeps me full between breakfast and dinner and it's very healthy and tasty. I like vanilla and pumpkin flavors, but you can use any combination of yogurt and granola flavors to switch it up.

- When going grocery shopping, try to opt for the low-fat options if they're available. For example, pick skim milk over whole milk and 93% ground beef over 73% ground beef. Also try to stick to natural foods instead of processed foods. For example, switching low-fat milk for whole milk can be effective because your body will still get calcium. You can also switch to Almond Milk, which is one of my favorites! It stays fresh for months at a time, tastes great, is healthy, and can be substituted for milk products quite easily.

- Invest in a small kitchen scale and a measuring cup set to help measure your meal proportions. Even though you can pretty much eat all the fruits and vegetables that you want without harming your body, it is easy to go overboard on things like cheese, meat, and pasta.

When creating a diet plan, a good idea is to create your own menu. You can research recipes and figure out what works best for you but it helps to have an idea what you're going to eat ahead of time. You can save yourself time, money, and health by planning ahead and making great eating choices.

Incorporating Exercise Into Your Diet Plan

It is important to remember that a diet plan will generally not work unless you're exercising at the same time. Exercising while you are dieting is very important because it helps your body burn fat. It also makes your bones, muscles, joints, lungs and other important body parts healthy and strong. Many people mistakenly believe they can eat poorly and then exercise to make up for it. In reality, junk food is so horrible for your body that it can take hours and hours of exercise just to burn it off, that is, if you can find the energy to do so after such poor eating choices. By eating healthy in the first place, you can lose weight quicker, keep it off and your overall health and energy levels will be much better.

The best types of exercises to engage in while dieting are **cardio** and **strength training**. In a nutshell, cardio helps you improve the way your lungs and heart function and strength training helps build your muscles and metabolism. Dieting alone can tend to make your metabolism slow down, so exercising regularly can help keep it up. The best way to get into the habit of exercising while dieting is to form a regular exercise routine.

It is important to remember that you should **start out slow** when you're first starting out. Don't try to go crazy on your first day of exercising, otherwise you will most likely tire yourself out, get injured, or be so sore the next day that you won't want to stick with it. If you're new to exercise, begin with something simple, like walking, and work your way up to more intense workouts.

A good way to know when to step up your training program is when you've gotten comfortable doing one type of exercise. Look at it as a challenge—when you've gotten used to walking, maybe try jogging, and then upgrade to running. You may be sore after the first couple rounds of exercising but as long as you stay consistent, there is a good chance that you will eventually feel so great that you won't want to stop exercising. I get exercise into my schedule each day. I start out slow by stretching and warming up, and then gradually build up the intensity. It is generally best, on a strength training day, to do the strength training first followed by the cardio work; this gives optimal results.

Staying Motivated While Dieting and Exercising

Dieting and exercising are not easy because it involves changing your lifestyle and many people are afraid of change. However, not all change is bad, especially if you are changing your diet; you're probably changing it for the better. By establishing a solid foundation of self-discipline and willpower for yourself, while incorporating a solid strategy, you can make the change to a healthier diet much easier. Did you know that making healthy choices can even help you enhance your willpower?

You can also enhance your willpower by adding plenty of wheat and whole-grain options to your diet. Many grocery stores offer whole-grain options in breads, pastas, and other items, so always go for the healthier kind. You'll be doing your body a favor and over time you may find it easier to control your cravings. Fruits and vegetables are also helpful for fueling your body properly.

Practicing self-discipline is also essential when it comes to dieting and living a healthy lifestyle. Obviously, it takes a lot of self-discipline to pass over junk food or to get up off the couch and exercise. Self-Discipline is often fueled by willpower, so as long as you focus on eating right, it shouldn't be too hard to get into the habit.

One good way to start practicing self-discipline in your everyday life is to make one change at a time. For example, when it comes to changing your diet, don't dive headfirst into making a million changes at once. I started out by switching out white bread for whole-grain bread and later I started switching whole milk for almond milk; then, one by one, I replaced old eating habits with better ones. I got used to eating healthier much quicker than I expected. It is a little like working your way up the exercise ladder. As with dieting, a good way to practice and strengthen self-discipline is to create a plan and keep working it.

Finally, do not be discouraged if you take a step backward. Nobody is perfect and we all have given into temptation at some point in our lives. The key is to just reflect upon your mistakes and then work to prevent them next time. Having willpower and self-discipline can help make dieting much easier and it can also help you out in other areas of your life, such as handling money, your relationships, your working life and resisting the temptation to abuse harmful substances. Once you've mastered all of these, then you really can feel at your best and be in a better position to achieve success. You will discover more of the benefits of exerting willpower and self-discipline in a few chapters.

Vitamins, Minerals, and Supplements

Every day, your blood flows through your body to your brain, your brain sends signals to other parts of your body, and your organs work to keep you alive. These are just some of the everyday functions of your body. However, for your body to work properly, it needs resources. If you are not properly taking care of your body it will be hard to achieve success. While your body can naturally produce some of the resources it needs to function, you can provide your body with the rest through your diet and supplements. You can do this by eating foods that are packed with vitamins and minerals as well as by trying different vitamins, minerals, and supplements.

Together, vitamins and minerals can help strengthen your bones, heal your injuries, and boost your immune system. They are also what helps your body convert food into energy and repair damage to cells. If your body goes too long without receiving the proper amount of vitamins and nutrients, it is possible to develop scurvy, blindness, rickets, or other very unpleasant conditions.

Using Supplements

A healthy, balanced diet should be your primary source of vitamins and minerals. However, some peoples' bodies are unable to function properly due to age or other medical factors. For example, pregnant women tend to need extra doses of certain nutrients and seniors' bodies often have trouble absorbing nutrients. Other peoples' bodies sometimes have a general deficiency. In situations like these, it is possible to take a dietary supplement to manually provide your body with the right amount of nutrients. Most vitamins and minerals come in the form of an over-the-counter supplement that you can buy in your local pharmacy, online or at your local health store. As always, you should always consult with your doctor about any new vitamins, minerals, or supplements you are taking.

I have personally been taking vitamins, minerals and a variety of supplements for the last twenty-five years. While there are all sorts of studies out about vitamins and minerals, I have had an overall good experience with them. When I look around and see other people around my age (just over forty), the difference is quite striking. I look younger, I am much stronger, I still have lightning quick reflexes, my skin looks healthy, I still have incredible mental capabilities, and I possess an overall good physical well-being. Although I'm not a doctor, I think one of the best decisions of my life was to invest in myself, which included a lot of healthy supplements and vitamins over the years. Of course you have to keep up with exercise and strength training as well.

My strategy has been to just give my body all the nutrients it needs in order for it to perform at peak performance. Over time you find out which vitamins and minerals and supplements work best for you, and discontinue taking the items that may not be having the desired effects. My cabinets are filled with vitamins, minerals, and a variety of other healthy supplements that you will see listed in this book. I try not to take too many at one time. I have found that four smaller meals per day works perfect for me, and I usually will take no more than around two to four different supplements after each meal. I have also found it beneficial to take days off from supplementation and to drink lots of water on those days.

Here are some of the best and most popular supplements that you can buy:

- Biotin (Vitamin B7)

- Folic Acid (Vitamin B9)

- Niacin (Vitamin B3)
- Riboflavin (Vitamin B2)
- Thiamin (Vitamin B1)
- Vitamin B6
- Vitamin B12
- Vitamin C
- Vitamin A
- Vitamin D
- Vitamin E
- Vitamin K
- Calcium
- Magnesium
- Phosphorus
- Potassium
- Sodium
- Chromium
- Copper
- Fluoride
- Iodine
- Iron
- Manganese
- Molybdenum

- Selenium

- Zinc

- Omega-3 Fatty Acids

A Good Night's Sleep

When you're constantly on the go, as many people are today, it is sometimes hard to keep yourself energized. Artificial energy drinks and candy bars easily tempt us as quick, cheap and easy ways to stay energized. I used to use them all the time as my main source of energy, when I was on the go. However, they did not seem to have a positive effect on me. While I enjoyed the initial surge of energy, I often found myself crashing and was even more tired and dehydrated later on. Sometimes it would take me a full day or two to recover from just one day of sodas, energy drinks, and other quick energy sources. While I was able to get a lot done in the initial burst of energy, I could have been much more productive and healthy over the long term if I had just done things right. I have discovered that the best ways to keep your body full of energy is to use all-natural products and remedies.

We all lead busy lives. No matter what kind of life you have, you probably have many responsibilities. If you're a businessperson, chances are that you are constantly thinking about your business, your clients and the work that you have to do. If you're a parent, you probably use most of your time cleaning, cooking and looking after your kids. Everyone's lives are different but one thing that we all have in common is a limited amount of time. Our many responsibilities often cause us to put a good night's sleep on the back burner. This is the first mistake that many people tend to make. Sleep is a very important step to living healthy and successful days.

Sleep allows your brain cells and other body cells to rest and charge back up for the next day. Your body also releases healthy hormones while your brain and cells rest. Although many of us believe that eight hours is the standard for sleeping, the amount of time needed for a good night's sleep actually depends on our age. While babies need the most amount of time for sleep (sixteen hours), toddlers and adolescents aged three to twelve usually only need ten or so hours of sleep. Many doctors recommend eight hours of sleep for those aged nineteen to fifty-five and people over sixty-five usually only need six hours of sleep. Surprisingly, 71% of people have reported that they do not get a standard amount of sleep and are actually sleep deprived.

If you consider yourself one of those people who do not get a good night's sleep, there are several steps you can take to change that. The first step in making sure you get enough sleep is to make sure your bedding is right for you. Make sure that your pillow is <u>firm</u> and <u>supports your head</u>. Some pillows can aggravate your allergies because of the filling or dust mites that build up on the surface, which can disrupt the amount of sleep you may get. If you are allergic to the stuffing in your pillow, a non-allergenic pillow might be a good option for you. If you are happy with the pillow that you have, I recommend changing pillow cases weekly.

A second step that you can take to get a good night's sleep is to **expose yourself to more light** during the day. Make it a habit to open your shades as soon as you wake up to let the sun shine through. Try not to wear sunglasses during the day and spend whatever time you can outside. For example, you can gain more exposure to more light by eating your lunch outside or taking a short morning walk. If you absolutely cannot spend much time outside (or if it's too cold out) you can keep your blinds and shades open to let more sunlight into your house or, if you spend a lot of time at work, you could try to move your desk closer to a window. Another option is to use a light therapy box as a way to get a good amount of light exposure.

Although more exposure to light during the day is good for getting enough sleep, you should also take steps to get less exposure to light at night, especially when you're getting ready for bed. At night, your body produces melatonin, a natural hormone that helps you fall asleep. Too much light exposure affects how much melatonin your body produces. You can help your body produce more melatonin by turning off all electronics at night, including your computers and televisions, reading from physical books instead of e-readers (the back light will affect your body's production of melatonin) and by turning off all your lights. If you are the type of person who likes to fall asleep with the television on in the background, try substituting for it some soft music or a "book on tape."

It is also a great idea to have a comfortable bed. I have slept on a **Select Comfort Air Bed** for over seven years and it is awesome. I sleep great and wake up with no neck or back pain. I have tried all sorts of mattresses and I think the air beds are by far the best.

A good night's sleep is a key step for feeling more energized. More energy gained from sleeping will make you more productive, sharp and emotionally settled during the day. If you are unable to get a good night's sleep, (for example, if you're awakened in the middle of the night due to an emergency) one way to make up for lost sleep is to take a mid-day nap. Not only is sleep great for re-energizing yourself, but it also protects you from other health issues by boosting your immune system. Some newer studies have shown that sleep deprivation may lead to heart disease, diabetes, and other diseases.

Chapter 4: Productivity and Self-Discipline

People who are productive and are able to exert a strong sense of self-discipline are often more likely to be successful. The more productive you can be in one day, the more likely you are to be successful out of all your peers. However, this is not easy and will certainly take a great amount of self-discipline. This chapter is all about these two topics, as well as subtopics of influence, willpower and persuasion. You will also learn about the best productivity habits that you can use to propel yourself toward success.

Influence

Influencing others and persuading those around you are two skills that you should master when trying to achieve success. Some of the greatest leaders and people in history have had this ability, and they have been remembered throughout the centuries because of it. There are different kinds of influence and persuasion techniques you can try to get the results you want. Don't forget, many of these techniques can be applied to yourself, as well as to others.

According to the Free Online Dictionary, influence can be defined as "a power affecting a person, thing, or course of events, especially one that operates without any direct or apparent effort: relaxed under the influence of the music; the influence of television on modern life."

Influence is all around you today. It is in the television, radio, internet, billboards, magazines, newspapers, books, people, and much more. Everything we look at and everything we hear influences our opinions and the choices we make. With all these messages bombarding us at every turn, it's easy to forget that, we too, are capable of influencing the decision making of ourselves and others.

If you master the skill of influencing yourself and others, it is only natural that the world will begin to reshape itself around you. It will begin to be full of more things that bring you joy and filled with fewer things that make you unhappy. So now that you know just how powerful influence can be, let's take a look at bringing more of it into your life.

The first technique will teach you how to make others feel valued by giving them recognition and involving them in decision making processes. Let's call this empowerment. Empowerment not only allows you to access other people's thoughts and opinions—what makes them tick—it also gives you the opportunity to discuss your way of thinking in an open and honest dialogue. When a decision is reached, the recognition you give to others for their involvement will make them more likely to reinforce your opinions the next time a decision comes up.

The second technique is to position your own ideas so that they meet the other person's concerns. The reason this is important is that it makes people feel valued.

Once a person feels valued by you, they are much more open to other ideas, persuasion methods, or knowledge you may wish to utilize or share.

When relating this to yourself, you should take a look at your own concerns about the problem at hand so that you can do more research on them. Once you have done your research, you can eliminate any unfounded concerns you may have had, or use your new knowledge to implement a better strategy for accomplishing your desired goal. It is a good idea to write down all your concerns on a piece of paper, and then systematically work your way through them, researching and taking notes as you go along. Once this is done, clearly write out the best strategy you can come up with to most effectively get the task or goal accomplished. It is also more compelling if you make this into a goal for yourself and set a deadline. Many famous people and peak performers have a written down lists of goals for themselves and will read through them daily. Some will also visualize themselves accomplishing their goal over and over again in vivid detail in their mind to really increase their chances of goal accomplishment. It is also a good idea to make the goal seem easy when writing it down. For example, instead of writing that I will stop watching too much television, I write that I will *easily* stop watching too much television and focus more of my time and energy on working out.

Another great influencing and persuasive technique involves bargaining with people, or with yourself. You can gain support from others by exchanging resources or favors. Think of this as a mutually rewarding experience. For example, if you like watching comedy movies and your partner likes action films, you can offer to reward your partner by saying that you'll watch two action movies with them next time if they let you right now watch that comedy film you've been dying to see.

In a business situation, you could offer to share some valuable information on an important subject in exchange for some other valuable information or service that would benefit you in your business or work environment. Bargaining is also a matter of give and take. If you want to keep someone in your life as a valuable ally, then it will be important that they feel happy in their transactions with you. Similarly, if you are the one doing all the giving and the other person is only take, take, take, then this is a great time to find new friends. Building relationships with others involves listening to them and getting to know them. Maintaining solid and friendly communications with a new friend will let them know that you like them and are open to their ideas. Once they feel trusted and appreciated by you, then the majority of people will also be open to your ideas and ways of thinking. As you know, your reputation is vitally important in business and in life. Building trust is an important part of your reputation.

You can also apply bargaining to yourself. If you're trying desperately to lose weight, and are dreaming of eating some very unhealthy and high calorie food, then tell yourself that if you don't give in and instead eat some healthier foods for the next few days, then you will treat yourself to a nice massage at the end of the week.

Particularly in the world of business, one of the keys to persuasive success is to find out who the key influencers are in your workplace. Using some of the strategies I have already discussed, you can potentially put yourself in the position of influencing the influencers. This is great when it comes to promotions, as you can exert your influence upon the influencer to let them know just how much you want the promotion and how hard you would be willing to work once it was granted. A few good words from the influencer could be all that is needed to tip the scales in your favor. Once you have a degree of persuasive ability with an influencer, be sure to nourish this relationship, as it could pay huge dividends for you in a variety of other situations that pop up for you in the future.

A great way to strengthen a relationship is to show the person that you share a common goal or vision. Sharing common visions with others is a powerful persuasive tool in its own right, but it also supplements other strategies such as relationship building. Common goals unite people, and the more united people feel with you, the more likely they will be to back up your ideas or to help you in a time of need.

Another good way to persuade people is with logic. Present a person with an inalienable truth he or she can't disagree with. Make sure you have your facts right, and the data to back it up and you leave them with little room to argue.

Another incredible way to build rapport with people is to mirror them. This technique makes the other person feel that the two of you are similar. When this happens, it is much easier for that person to like you and trust you. For example, if someone likes to talk extremely loudly all the time, then talk back to him in a loud voice. If she is shy and talks very softly, talk very calmly and softly back to them. If his arms are crossed, you can casually cross your arms. If her legs are crossed, go ahead and cross your legs. If he likes to smile a lot, smile right back at him. If she is very serious with a harsh tone, be serious right back to her with just as harsh a tone. Almost nobody is going to notice that you are mirroring them unless you take it too far. This is an incredible technique that will help you make friends and increase your influence.

So far, you've discovered positive strategies to persuade people. But some people choose to employ more negative persuasion techniques. Many people choose to persuade others by acting as dramatic as possible. Crocodile tears, screaming, guilt trips, and temper tantrums are a few such tactics. When techniques such as these are being used against you, it is important that you maintain an emotional distance. Do not let yourself be drawn into a negative situation or influenced into making a hasty decision you will soon regret. When you give in to situations like these, it only reinforces the other person's bad behavior, making it a tactic that person will more than likely use on you in future situations. You need to be strong and make the best decision for your own personal goals and dreams. When a person's negative behavior does not give the desired result, it will usually stop happening.

Persuasion

Now you know some great ways to influence people. But how do you persuade them if your influencing tactics haven't worked? Is it doable? You bet it is! People are doing it to you all the time.

Turn on the TV. Go ahead. Find a channel that's cut to a commercial break. Now watch one of the commercials. What did that commercial do? It tried to persuade you to buy that product, or donate to that charity, or something else advertisers wanted you to do. Did it work?

- **How did they try to persuade you?**

    First of all, many commercials will focus on what's in it for you. They do this by demonstrating what may be missing from your life, or how your life would be greatly improved by their product. Perhaps there is a new dish detergent that moistens your skin instead of dehydrating it while you're washing the dishes, or maybe you've been shown how to keep your computer clean from viruses just by using their product. More than likely, you'll be given examples of how their product has worked for thousands of people, just like you, or how nine out of ten doctors recommend this product over the competitor's.

    After they tell you all of the different ways the product can benefit you, then you will usually be bombarded with facts, testimonials, and figures to back up their claims.

    Finally, don't forget that this particular offer is limited to the first one hundred callers or only for customers who buy now. In essence, you'll have been shown that the product is in short supply, so you must hurry. This technique makes the product seem more valuable than it actually is because of an implied scarcity.

    So let's list those steps and discuss how you can use each one to persuade other people. Let's do this by supposing that Janet wants to persuade her husband Jack to buy a new car, while Jack, is reluctant to take out another loan to cover the cost of a new vehicle. He believes that their current vehicles are just fine.

- **Focus on the other party's need**

    Make sure they know what is missing from their lives, or how their lives may be drastically improved by having the product.

    Janet starts out by telling Jack that the new car comes with a 100,000 mile warranty, and that all repair costs are covered by the manufacturer, not just labor. She continues by telling Jack that he wouldn't need to spend so much time on the weekends performing maintenance and fixing the car because scheduled servicing is also included. She finishes by telling Jack that they could spend more time together doing the things that they enjoy rather than her watching him underneath the car all weekend.

- **Tell how it has worked for others**

Janet tells Jack that George and Mildred next door bought a new car and it has saved them thousands in gas mileage and servicing costs; that Mildred said it drives like a dream, even in the snow which, Janet tells Jack, is something she has been concerned about for a while now.

- **Back up the product with facts and figures**

Before presenting her idea to Jack, Janet has done a bit of homework and found that the insurance on the new car is hundreds of dollars cheaper per year than on her old one. Not only that, but by the time you calculate in servicing costs, gas mileage costs, and annual repair bills, it would actually save them some money over the course of the next several years. In addition, the local dealership is offering low cost financing that would further decrease costs.

- **Make sure they know that your offer is limited; this increases its perceived value**

Janet lets Jack know that the low cost financing deal is only running until the end of the week, and that after that, the finance cost will be nearly double what the dealership is offering right now. Also, if they use Janet's old car as a trade in, the dealership is offering a three-thousand dollar instant rebate along with a hefty discount off the car's sticker price. Knowing that Jack's a huge football fan, she says that with that kind of cash they could afford a two week vacation right around the time of the Super Bowl!

Poor Jack really didn't stand a chance, did he? Although this example is a bit stereotypical and completely fictional, it does show the steps of persuasion in action.

Fuel Your Willpower

The American Psychological Association defines willpower as "the ability to resist short-term temptations in order to meet long-term goals." Many people consider their lack of willpower to be the number one reason why they fail at such things such as learning new skills, quitting smoking, and losing weight, among other things. When we feel that we have a lack of willpower, we feel like we are 'weak' individuals, and use this weakness to talk ourselves out of putting in the work necessary to accomplish our goals. Once you have gotten in the habit of quitting and giving up, it gets easier and easier to put things off and make excuses instead of doing what really needs to get done. Winners tend to have a strong willpower and are less likely to give up, even if it takes them several attempts. Losers are more likely to give up on the first try or two without exercising much willpower.

There have been several studies designed to find out whether willpower is a resource that different people have at different levels, and whether this precious resource is only available to us in limited amounts. You may be surprised to learn that these studies did indeed find that willpower is a limited resource: You only have so much of it to spend on accomplishing your given goals. Once this resource is depleted, we are almost certain to fail in accomplishing our desired goal.

Let's continue with the idea that willpower is a limited resource. Like any resource, it can be depleted and restored. Think of it like planting two trees every time you cut one down, or going to the gas station to fill up your car when the fuel tank is low. If you think about willpower in these terms, then it is possible for you to do certain things that will help restore low levels of willpower and to also do certain things to ensure your willpower remains strong over long periods of time. After all, if you plant two trees for every one you cut down, you are increasing the world's resource pool. Likewise, you can fill up emergency gas containers to store in your car and use them if the need should arise.

Studies have shown that people who have low blood glucose levels have smaller reserves of willpower than people with typical levels of glucose in their bloodstream. While this is important in fuelling your willpower levels, it is equally important not to allow your blood glucose levels to become too high. High blood glucose levels have been linked to obesity, heart disease, pre-diabetes, and diabetes. So, what are the best ways to maintain a healthy blood glucose level?

The first thing to do is cut down on foods that are filled with sugar. And yes, you're right: This will take willpower. However, the small expenditure of willpower you spend on resisting the sugary snack is nothing compared to how much willpower you'll build as your body rids itself of all that refined sugar and the empty calories of carbohydrates. You'll also notice that your energy levels improve as your body becomes less dependent on refined sugars and caffeine. Your energy will become more stable as opposed to the energy bursts and crashes that come with consuming sugary foods and drinks. With increased energy, it becomes much easier to exert your willpower effectively.

Another great way to maintain a healthy blood glucose level is to always choose a whole-grain option when it is available to you. Most grocery stores carry whole-grain versions of breads, pastas, rice and cereals. This should be an easy switch for anyone. Quite simply, whole-grain foods taste better than their refined counterparts, and will leave you feeling fuller for longer. It is also easier for you to resist snacking on sugary treats throughout the day when you are not hungry. A quick final note: Check the labels on cereals that advertise themselves as whole-grain. While it is great to have whole-grain cereal, many of these products also contain huge amounts of refined sugar.

Massively important in the effort to rebuild and increase your resource pool of willpower is eating a good dose of fruits and vegetables. Try choosing to eat an apple over that high sugar candy bar. The energy you get from apples will last longer than the energy from a candy bar, and you won't experience a sugar crash after the initial burst of sugar-based energy. You can also try eating oranges instead of drinking orange juice. They're lower in calories, help fight hunger pangs and give you an energy boost, all at the same time they're delivering vital vitamins and minerals into your body.

A good mood has been shown to have a direct influence on your levels of willpower. Being in a positive mood gives you more energy and inspiration to accomplish your goals that require willpower. Let's think about this for a moment. If you are feeling good after watching a life-affirming movie, for instance, you are much more likely to make some positive choices in your actions for the next few days. It's similar to the effect that can be gained from attending a twelve-step recovery meeting: You leave the meeting with a positive mindset (recovery is possible) and with the goal to make more positive choices (I don't need that drink/drugs/etc. to be happy).

So how do you recreate positive feelings in day-to-day life?

Having a positive self-image goes a long way in enabling us to build up increasingly higher levels of willpower. As you are bombarded every day by images of supermodels and beautiful people, you need to be realistic about your body image. You can strive for greatness, but don't get too overly concerned about it to the extent that it will limit your success potential. There are millions of success stories about average looking people going on to achieve incredible things. Many people who may not be athletic or the best looking use this as fuel to work even that much harder than everyone else to ensure their success.

Self-acceptance is a great way to build a positive self-image. You're not perfect. Get over it. We all have our flaws, and we all have things that we're good at. What's important is that we are making a good strategic plan and doing our best to accomplish it as effectively as possible, helping ourselves and other people along the way. Take every opportunity to give yourself credit for all the hard work and great things that you have done in your life. Keeping a diary is also a good idea. Be sure to write down or voice record the good things that happen in your life. It is always fun to sit down and read them or play them back years later when you may be feeling down.

Productivity and Success

Productivity is very important and it has many definitions. I like to view productivity as what we get when we divide value by time. Technically speaking, there are two ways of looking at productivity. If you can get good value from spending a lot of time on a task, then you have achieved productivity and if you can complete one or more tasks quickly then you've just added a valuable resource to your day—time. Most importantly, the sooner you start saving time, the more you can accomplish during your lifespan. More procrastination equals more wasted time. Being productive is important for everyone. Whether you are a businessperson, a student, or you work from home, productivity is a very important factor in your life.

Good Habits for Productivity

1. **Learn Time Management Skills**

By getting into some routine, productivity-improving habits, you can increase your productivity, both at work and at home. Some of these habits are good for increasing productivity in the short-term, but if you maintain them, these habits will serve you well for years to come. Having good time management skills is one of the best productivity-boosting habits you can adopt. When you are able to prioritize your time, you will find yourself able to better manage your tasks and you might even come out with some free time for yourself, once you get really good at it.

The first step to learning how to manage your time is to realize the value and importance of time. Then, you should become aware of how much time you spend on each of your tasks. If you are working on a task that you've never done before, make a note of what time you start and set a deadline for yourself. If you are working on tasks you are familiar with, you will learn as you do them how long they take you and they will become easier to manage over time. All in all, there are many ways to practice good time management skills; the more you practice them, the sooner they will become second-nature to you.

2. **Ask For Help**

Whether at home or at work, nobody should have to do everything themselves. For example, if you are a manager, you shouldn't be afraid to delegate some of your tasks to your co-workers. You can also ask friends and family for help. Asking for help usually enables you to get the job done twice as fast and leaves you with more time and energy to devote to other activities. Many people do not ask others for help because of trust issues or shyness. Many people do not trust others to complete a task as well as they can do it themselves. Others are often simply too shy to ask, hoping someone will read their minds and volunteer to help. In most cases they will end up hoping for help that never comes. If you decide to ask someone for help as a way to improve your productivity, pick someone in whom you have the utmost confidence, someone you can count on to complete what they promise, and someone you feel comfortable asking. Be sure to return the favor; reciprocity in helping can build strong bonds among friends and render you much more productive in the long run.

3. **Take a Break**

For those of you who sit at a desk for most of the day, you may notice that your energy levels easily drain. This is because your fat cells tend to build up in your bodies when you sit for a long time. Fat cells drain you of your energy, making you less productive. It also generally has a negative impact on your health. One good way to stay energized throughout your work day is to take a break from sitting down. Get up, walk around and let your mind clear from your work. At home, it is also good to take breaks. If you do so much work at home that your mind begins to fog, do the same: get up, take a walk or do something fun, and let your mind rejuvenate.

It is never a good idea to focus on one task for too long—your mind and body will eventually get drained out and you will not perform as well or as fast as you would without giving it a rest. You can utilize your break time to eat a healthy snack, take a brisk walk, take a nap, listen to a hypnosis download or do something else that will complement your productivity.

4. Focus and Avoid Interruptions

The best method to get things done is to try and focus on one task at a time, especially if your tasks are not related. You should also stay working on it until it's completely finished. Again, turn off all distractions to make this habit easier. If you switch between too many tasks without finishing them, it is easier to become disappointed and confused; you may forget important points of each task. A good way to stay on track is to avoid interruptions. You can avoid interruptions by simply closing your office door, turning off your phone or just ignoring other distractions while you focus on what is most important. Studies show that when you are interrupted from doing something, you risk an 80% chance of not getting back to it at all.

Learning to say no also can help increase your productivity. Saying no is not easy, especially when it comes to close friends, family and bosses, yet sometimes you have to bite the bullet and do it. However, saying no doesn't have to be a dreadful thing. For example, if somebody calls and asks you to hang out while you are working, do not give in to temptation—simply reschedule the request. It will save you time, help you focus, and it will motivate you to get your tasks done because it gives you something to look forward to.

5. Follow Up On Your Goals

Most of us are aware that goal-setting is easy—actually going through with achieving your goals is the hard part. Distractions and overall laziness often tempt us to state our goals and then put them off until a later date. By taking immediate action to work toward your goals, you will have a better chance at achieving them. You should also read through your goals every day! Making excuses is a common flaw that many of us tend to have but you can overcome it by actively taking steps toward your goals. Instead of wishing that you could do something, just put your fears aside and do it.

Give yourself a head start. Even if you are unsure about how well your goals are planned out—you can always flesh out your goals along the way. Following up on your goals will make you more productive, because the more you get done, the more you learn and can apply to multiple areas of your life.

For example, if you wish you could learn a new language, do something about it: take a class or buy some language-learning software. Then, make a commitment to it and follow through. Once you successfully learn the language, you can use it to help other people with translations, you can travel to a country where it is the main language, and you can add it to your resume, which may increase your chances at getting a new or better job. The possibilities are endless when you follow up on your goals.

If you are truly serious about accomplishing a goal, tell other people about it who you respect. It is always extremely disappointing to tell people you care about and respect that you have failed, so this can serve as a strong motivator to accomplish your goal. For many, just the shame of failing will motivate them to succeed; if that doesn't affect you, you can always assign yourself a penalty for failure, collected by your accountability partner. This is basic, but it can definitely motivate.

6. Give Yourself a Reward

Finally, there is nothing better than getting something nice for working hard all week. Rewarding yourself for hard work gives you something to look forward to and will help motivate you to get all of your work done. It is similar to taking a break, but your reward can be a little bigger. Remember when you unplugged your TV and disabled your social media profiles? Allow yourself to reconnect to these things when you have completed all the work you need to get done or after you've reached one of your goals. If you want to really reward yourself, you could plan a trip or vacation for you and your family, which will net you quality family time and a relaxing break from your regular work.

7. Fill in Time Gaps

One way to seriously boost your productivity is to fill in any time gaps that you have. Time gaps are miscellaneous periods of time that are too short to get an entire task done but long enough to do something productive. For example, if you are waiting for a client to call you back after your conversation is interrupted, use that spare time to read up on something or to prepare your next big task. You will be surprised at how much more you can get done when you utilize all of the time gaps throughout your day.

8. Monitor Yourself

By monitoring your goals and your progress toward them, you can easily keep track of your performance. This strategy can be short-term or long-term. Monitor your goals at work and at home by keeping track of reports, reviews or by keeping your own notes. You can incorporate the habit of following up on your goals as a main motivator to keep track of your performance. By reviewing your goals on a regular basis, you can analyze your progress to see where you need to make changes and where you are excelling. Reviewing goals daily is an excellent habit, practiced by many of the greatest people in the world.

9. Differentiate Between "Perfect" and "Complete"

Many people are perfectionists but they do not realize how much of a time-waster perfectionism can be. Contrary to popular belief, perfectionism does not always drive successful results. A fully completed project will almost always get better results than a perfect but incomplete project. You should also learn to differentiate between perfect results and polished results. You can always go back and edit, update or revise your project or task.

If you cannot go back and change things, then it is important that you do a quality job the first time. While it is advantageous in some instances to just get a project completed, if lack of perfection will hurt your reputation, then it is better to ensure the task is done correctly the first time.

I personally lean towards more of a perfectionist standard. While this can be time consuming, I get incredible joy when a project is finished, knowing that it will stand the test of time.

10. Set Deadlines and Appropriate Standards

Setting a deadline is a very effective strategy for increasing productivity. When you have a deadline for a project or a task, you are aware of when you need to finish it and how long you have to finish it. Without a deadline, it is easy for you to forget about projects and tasks and it's even easier for you to put them off. Also, try to set appropriate standards for your task. Do not try to associate your task with high, unreachable standards. Set the standards at a realistic and reachable rate. You can supplement this strategy with the habit of writing a to-do list or keeping a planner to help you keep track of your deadlines.

11. Break up Large Tasks

If you have a really big task and you cannot get help from anyone, try to break it down into smaller tasks. This way, you will not get overwhelmed by the stress of facing the whole project at once. You also avoid burning out all your mental energy as a result of feeling overwhelmed by the enormity of the entire task. To accomplish this an author, for example, might write a book one chapter at a time until he or she is done; a home builder will just focus on one stage of a building project at a time; a world class athlete will focus on one workout or one set of exercises at a time. Breaking up large tasks into smaller subtasks involves combining the skills of using a to-do list/planner with time management strategies, and plans for keeping up your energy and continually feeding yourself inspiration and motivation.

12. Don't Rush

Finally, don't rush through anything. Trying to get things done too fast may generate negative results. Your work quality may suffer if you try to fly through a task too quickly. Speed can also cause stress and anxiety, which can actually drain your mental energy and make you less productive. A good way to pace yourself is to tackle one task at a time. Do the most important things first and save the least important ones for last. Saving the least important items for last also can serve as an incentive, because you will not have to work as hard in the end.

Chapter 5: Conquer Fear and Be Confident!

The ability to display ultimate self-confidence and to conquer your fears will help get you on the fast track to success. While these two areas are hard for some people to achieve, they are definitely not impossible. In this chapter, you will discover some great ways to boost your self-confidence as well as some great techniques on how to overcome your fears.

Self-confidence is a personal attitude that goes hand-in-hand with having a positive and realistic view of yourself. When you have a high level of self-confidence, you tend to have better control over your life, a better ability to trust your own senses and a better ability to believe in yourself. On that note, do not mistake having a high level of self-confidence for having the ability to do *everything*. The key to remember is that having lots of self-confidence requires being realistic; even when you cannot reach a goal or get something accomplished, you can still maintain a positive outlook.

How to Boost Your Self-Confidence

- **Reflect on Positive Experiences.** Many people with low self-esteem tend to wallow on negative past experiences. By **thinking about times when you felt your greatest**, you can use the past to push yourself forward into the future. For example, think about a time when you accomplished something wonderful at work. Can you remember how good it felt and what you did to get there? Remind yourself that you can have that feeling again as you complete your current objective. By doing this, your chances of feeling more confident in the moment can increase. It's also a good idea to maintain a journal and make a written record of your favorite positive life experiences. You can include pictures, awards, events, friends or anything that makes you happy. Then, be sure and review parts of this journal a couple of times a week to keep your spirits high.

- **"Stop" Negative Thoughts.** Learn how to become more aware of when you start thinking negatively and then say "**stop**," either out loud or internally. Many therapists use this technique and you can do it yourself, anywhere. This can prevent you from getting too wrapped up in negative emotions that can bring down your self-confidence. To learn some awesome and easy do-it-yourself techniques on how to stop thinking negatively, I invite you to check out this YouTube video, Negative Thoughts: How to Stop Negative Thoughts, Fear, Stress & Self-Doubt by Nathaniel Solace.

- **Practice Good Posture.** When you slouch or slump over, you are essentially sending a message to other people that you have low self-esteem. In turn, this could deter people from approaching you, which may in turn, cause you to feel less confident in social interactions. When you practice good posture, by standing tall and strong and sitting straight in your chair, it shows that you are proud of yourself; it may actually make you more approachable. When you stand and sit tall, it helps you feel important internally. Be sure to practice making eye contact and keeping your head up, too. For a good video on how to practice good posture, check out this helpful YouTube Video: <u>How to Get Good Posture</u> by Posture Confidence.

- **Dress Well.** The way you dress often says a lot about you and can influence how you feel about yourself. By dressing well, you can make yourself look even better than you already are and you can feel more empowered. Although it may feel like others judge you by the way you dress, the person who judges you the most tends to be yourself. That said, you don't have to dress up in a suit or tie every day. Just try to avoid wearing dirty, wrinkled, ripped, or old clothing. Look presentable and well groomed.

- **Be Heard.** People who have low levels of self-confidence tend to stay quiet when they are in large groups. This usually happens out of a fear of being judged. However, this fear of judgement is often a misconception. Even by just speaking up once or twice every time you're around people, you can help yourself improve at public speaking; this, in turn, can really help you become more confident. For some very helpful tips on improving your public speaking skills, check out this informative YouTube video, <u>How to Speak Up Without Freaking Out</u> by Dice News. The video is aimed at people in a work environment, but you can apply the principles to other situations as well.

- **Be Humble.** Avoid bragging and other ego-inflating activities. Be humble and modest and you may feel more confident. When you act this way, your confidence can naturally shine through you and you won't have to put so much effort into trying to impress others.

Great Self-Confidence Exercises

- **Correct Interpretation.** At some point in your life, you have probably been the butt of a bad joke. Think about what you were feeling. Angry? Hurt? There's nothing worse than having a bunch of people laugh at you and feeling embarrassed or bad about yourself. However, you can sometimes prevent feeling that way if you correctly understand where the insult is coming from in the first place. Many times, you will encounter somebody who is purposefully trying to hurt your feelings. On the other hand, you may have some friends and family members who just like to tease and be sarcastic

    Usually, those types of people don't truly intend any harm. For example, if you're wearing a bright orange shirt, a friend might joke that you look like you're ready to go direct traffic. Now, your friend probably didn't mean that in a way other than to just try and be funny, but you might interpret it as a bash on your fashion sense. Research actually shows that people who are sarcastic and witty often mistakenly insult others because they do not think of the implications their jokes can have. If you are ever in a situation like that, the best thing to do would be to take a deep breath and ask yourself, "Does this person just have bad social skills?" or "Is this a situation that is okay for me to take lightly?"

- **Self-Talk.** The way you think and talk to yourself can have an important impact on how you act. One great way to boost your self-confidence is to learn how to talk to yourself in a way that can help drive you to make positive changes in your life. For example, if you are an introvert, you may think to yourself, "I am shy," when you're around groups of people. You probably feel nervous in those situations. In that case, you can change the way you talk to yourself to try and change your actions. For example, tell yourself how you *want* to be. Instead of saying, "I'm shy," tell yourself that you want to be friendly with others when you're in a group. By doing that, you may feel more encouraged to be interested in other people. You can apply this technique to any area of life in which you're not feeling confident. It's also a good idea to have a few favorite positive affirmations that you can think to yourself when you want to be more productive or just drown out any negative self-talk. Be sure to use some creativity, and come up with a few catch phrases that appeal to you and your goals.

- **Prepare Yourself for Pressure.** In life, it is pretty much impossible to avoid situations in which you're put under pressure. You are not often given much time to prepare for these situations. When these things happen, you may feel a blow to your confidence because you're not sure what to say or do. One great technique you can employ to avoid this is to plan out scenarios and how you're going to act. Here are some scenarios in which you can plan out what to think or say when you're in the moment:

    1. When your boss puts a rush on a task and you have no extra time.

    2. When a client or colleague who you are responsible for overseeing messes up.

    3. When a loved one asks you for a favor that you don't want to give.

    4. If one of your employees gives you endless excuses for making a mistake.

    5. Any other peer-pressure moment that you may want to avoid based off your personal life.

Overcome Fear and Strive toward Success

Fear is a part of our being when we are born and stays with us until death. This self-preservation reaction keeps us safe, but it can also hold us back from reaching success. Everyone has fears; it is how you deal with them that matters. Fear has a tendency to keep you stuck where you are and does not allow you to progress any further in your development until the fear is overcome. Someone who is afraid of lightning and thunder will continue to be afraid of it if they don't do something about it. They might hide in a closet or under their bed until the storm is over. They may miss an event like a family reunion or an outing with friends, merely because there is a chance of bad weather. This person is stuck, immobilized, and can easily miss out on enjoyable events as long as they give in to the fear.

Techniques for Overcoming Fear

- **Yoga** is the perfect exercise for reducing panic and fear. Yoga is a combination of breathing and movement. It is an ancient practice that melds together the body, mind and spirit. Breathing is very important in yoga because it prepares the brain to be calm. The different stretches and poses of yoga center the body and make it stronger and more balanced. Another aspect of yoga is meditation. Meditation is used to link the spirit to the mind and the body. Many practitioners run thorough a litany of mantras and positive affirmations while meditating, posing, and breathing and this can reinforce confidence and overcome fear. When you do your exercises, repeat your positive affirmations to banish fear. For example, if you are afraid of crowded areas, a good affirmation to repeat could be: "I enjoy being around others and people like me." The repetition of the mantra wiggles into the subconscious mind in a positive manner and you might find yourself gravitating towards crowded areas with no problems at all.

- **Breathing** is a great way to relax and help yourself focus on overcoming pain or any other horrible feeling. Deep breathing slows the heart rate, relaxes muscles, and helps concentration. Yogic breathing includes deep breathing and does similar things. Avoid breathing too quickly or overdoing it; this can cause hyperventilation, in which you feel like you are suffocating or are very light-headed.

    In one breathing exercise, you draw air across your tongue, which causes a cooling sensation that calms the nervous system. Do this while sitting in a chair or while sitting cross-legged on the floor.

- **Cool Breath Breathing Exercise:**

    1. Stick the tongue out of the mouth and curl the sides of it up. Your tongue should look like a roll or straw.
    2. Lift the chin up, pointing it towards the ceiling.
    3. Breathe in using the diagram, drawing air through the tongue.
    4. Hold the breath for a few seconds, uncurl the tongue, and move it back into the mouth.
    5. Exhale through the nostrils and move the chin down.

Do this exercise six times at first, but gradually increase the repetitions until you are completing the breathing cycle twelve times. The more practice you get in, the more this exercise will imprint upon your brain. After it has become an ingrained habit, this may become an almost automatic response to fear.

The YouTube video <u>Healing Through Yoga: Releasing Fear and Anxiety</u> by 4wholeness, shows how the stomach and abdomen look when you breathe from the diaphragm. It shows how the diaphragm moves out and in when you breathe correctly.

- **Tensing Exercise**

Another exercise where concentration is involved is the tensing exercise. When fear strikes, your muscles tend to involuntarily tense up. In the tensing exercise, you tense your muscles to simulate a fearful situation. Then you train yourself to gradually relax those muscles. In addition to physically releasing your fear, this exercise requires some concentration, which distracts the brain from the fear and allows it to relax.

1. Lie down flat on the floor or on a bed.
2. Breathe in deeply, using the diaphragm, then hold your breath.
3. Purposefully tense the muscles in your head, neck and shoulders and count to ten.
4. Let out your breath slowly, as you consciously relax the muscles in the neck and shoulders, starting with your neck and going from the shoulders to the upper arms.
5. Do the same with the arms and hands. Tense and relax from the upper arm down to the tips of the fingers.
6. Continue the tensing and release exercise down the trunk of your body, starting at the upper chest and working down toward the hips. Pay special attention to your stomach area.
7. Continue from the hips and buttocks down to your toes.

Perform the breathing and the tensing exercises once a day; whenever fear takes hold, begin them immediately. The breathing exercise should slow your fear-induced elevated heart rate. The tensing exercise should help reduce muscle tension. Both exercises work together to allow you to move your fear from the fight-or-flight instinctive brain to the cognitive parts of your brain, where it can be recognized as irrational.

Learn how to stop anxiety and fear in all kinds of situations, from human encounters to being stuck in an elevator. The techniques in the YouTube video, <u>How to Calm Down in 10 Seconds (Fast Relaxation Trick to Stop</u>

Anxiety and Stress) by ALifeLessAnxious include a great example of the breathing and tensing exercises.

If you can't seem to automatically start the breathing exercises, keep a regular, large sized blow up balloon in your pocket. When panic starts, take it out and blow it up. This will automatically stop swift breathing and can help alleviate the panic symptoms. Utilize breathing and tensing techniques whenever fear takes hold.

- **Physical Exercise**

Simply doing something physical like pushups, sit-ups or jumping jacks can also prevent fear from setting in. While you are doing these exercises, count the repetitions; this will help occupy your brain and divert it from thinking about your fear. Another good idea is to burn energy constructively by walking or cleaning the house.

The University of Georgia performed a study that analyzed forty clinical trials associated with medical and mental conditions. The study found that patients who participated in regular exercise sessions reduced their anxiety by about twenty percent. These patients had fewer symptoms of worry and fear than those who did not exercise. They also found that the patients who exercised regularly for thirty minutes or more per day were much more adept at reducing fear and anxiety by themselves. Physical exercise can help many people with overcoming fear.

Exercise also releases endorphins; these are hormones that make you feel good. Regular exercise releases these hormones, which can result in making you feel you can take on the world and conquer any fear. If you would like to know more about this, be sure to check out my bestselling book: Ultimate Health Secrets.

Chapter 6: Leadership and Team-Building

Leadership is a very valuable life skill. If you have excellent **leadership skills,** you are often more successful in both your work and personal lives. Your leadership skills can define your success in running your home, raising your family, influencing others, and earning your salary, along with many other important things. You may have found yourself believing that people are born with great leadership skills, but that's not necessarily true. Anybody can be a great leader! All it takes is the ability to learn and master the skills and knowledge behind great leadership. Leaders are the ones who face challenges head on and never give up until a solution is reached. In a broad sense, people with great leadership skills have the ability to change the world.

Leadership is important, whether you are influencing the world or just a small group of individuals. People with great leadership skills often climb the ladders at their jobs quicker, are more respected, make more money, and are more memorable than other people. If you are a parent and your leadership skills are weak, you may not find that your children are not behaving as well as you'd like them to. Students who are leaders often have better education prospects and often carry their leadership skills into the real world. In short, there are virtually no negatives to strengthening your leadership skills. Your life might be great right now, but the more you can develop as a leader, the better off you can be. Once you have mastered basic leadership skills, you may find yourself with the power and the opportunities to open more doors for yourself and others than you've ever thought possible.

Best Leadership Habits

1. **Be a Planner.** One great way to better manage your time and projects is to make a **plan**. Each morning, try to create a rough plan for the day in your head, on the computer, or on paper and then follow it. Without a good plan, you may find it easier to put off important tasks and waste a lot of precious time on trivialities.

2. **Assess Your Situation.** If you're strapped for time, take five minutes to step back from your daily operation and take an assessment. See if there is anything you can identify that might be taking more time than you originally planned for. (For example, if you're managing a restaurant, you might suddenly get hit with an unexpected rush that sets you back 20 minutes in your maintenance tasks.) Try to create a contingency plan for times that things do not work according to the original plan. As part of your assessment, you can also consider eliminating strategies that are not working and implementing something new that may allow things to run smoother.

3. **Think Proactively.** Thinking proactively can help you stay a couple of steps ahead, thus reducing the chances that you will run into problems in the future that could have been avoided. While some things can be prevented, try to be prepared for changes, surprises and obstacles. Preparing yourself in

advance for potential problems can help you stay calm in times of distress and help lead your team to success when these situations do arise.

4. **Be Adaptable.** As a leader, you will often be required to travel, meet new people and be ready to tackle unfamiliar situations. When you're not willing to change or go into unfamiliar situations with positive thoughts and energy, you could hinder your success potential as a leader. Practice adaptability and build it up for whenever you find yourself in a new situation. Things are not always going to go your way so, instead of throwing a fit, try to be adaptable and make the best of any given situation.

5. **Be Honest At All Times.** To be a leader in any situation, being honest at all times is crucial, because you need to have the respect and trust of others. Your level of honesty and integrity is a reflection of yourself and how others will perceive you. It builds good character and makes you a trustworthy and respected person. Finally, if you present yourself as an honest person, your employees will likely model your behavior. In business and in life, your reputation is everything.

6. **Have a Flexible Perspective.** A **flexible perspective** can help you open your mind to new leads and ideas. It can also help you stay ahead of the game by being able to see new connections and patterns in your market. Of course, you can still keep your old perspective, but a great leader knows when it is time to switch things up.

7. **Ask Questions.** Asking questions of yourself and your team is important for staying active and ahead of the game. What you want to do is ask the *right* questions. Instead of asking questions about problems, ask questions about solutions. For example, instead of asking, "*Why* haven't we made any breakthroughs yet?" say, "*What* problems do our customers have and how can we solve them?" Asking the right questions can make you a great, innovative leader. Some of the greatest solutions and inventions in history have been made by people who have been able to find the answer to this sentence: "There has got to be a better way to..."

8. **Write But Don't Send.** When you're angry at an employee or teammate, the last thing that you want to do is to lose your temper. A good strategy for releasing your negative thoughts toward somebody is to write an angry email but <u>don't</u> send it—instead, save it as a **draft** and then look at it again only after you've cooled off. Abraham Lincoln used to do this, except in letter format. This can save you the embarrassment of words you wish you hadn't said in the future. Of course there are always be situations where anger is justified and you may need to take more serious actions. However it is usually best to wait until you have had time to cool down and think the situation through before choosing your response.

9. **Practice Decision-Making Skills.** Decision-making in any situation can be difficult. Many people often find themselves in denial when they have to

make a big decision, often doing whatever it takes to put off making a commitment. Luckily, there are some great ways to simplify your **decision-making** and make it practical and effective. See if you can break down a troublesome decision into simple steps, and then analyze the consequences of each option for each step. If you have time, plan it out so that you have enough time to look at all of your options. Sometimes, making a bad decision can be better than making no decision at all. All great leaders have the ability to be decisive when needed.

10. **Apologize When You're Wrong.** When you've made a mistake or said something to someone and you know you were in the wrong, make it a point to genuinely apologize right away. Something as simple as saying you're sorry can be very effective. More often than not, the other person will be satisfied and you will be less stressed. It is tough to respect someone who will never admit when they're wrong.

11. **Be Resourceful.** As a leader, you will probably have many people coming to you with questions. As I have mentioned before, it is true that leaders do not always have an answer. However, if you can go and find out an answer to a question, it can make you a much more effective leader. The key here is to actually follow through on your promise; find out the answer and deliver it. As a leader, it is very easy to find out answers, with the internet right at your hands. Just be sure the answers are accurate.

12. **Reflect Daily and Create a Mission Statement.** Reflecting on yourself each day is a great way to relax, get in touch with yourself and your personal mission, and to gain personal feedback. Ponder questions such as, "What do I stand for?" "Who am I?" "How do I want to influence other people?" Ask yourself these and other similar questions as a way to create a personal mission and vision. Once you've figured out what motivates you and why you want to impact others, write it down and work on it a little each day until you slowly start crafting yourself into the leader that you've visualized.

You can use this technique to be a leader in any area of life, not just at work. The good news is that leading at home often increases your experience for leading people at work. Here is a good example of a personal mission statement that can be used for either your personal or work life:

I will learn how to balance my personal interests with my important responsibilities. I want others to see me as somebody to look up too, confide in and trust. I will achieve this by respecting the privacy of others and by instilling confidence in the people around me. I will set goals for where I want to be at the beginning of every week and share them with my peers. I will be honest and do all my work with full integrity, even if it means admitting my mistakes. I will strive to improve every day and be the best leader I can possibly be.

Your mission statement can be as long or short as you want and you can change it any time you feel the need, since it is completely yours. Reflect on your mission statement every day, or at least once a week, to ensure that you are leading others to the best of your abilities. Here are some more questions that you can ask yourself:

- Do I speak my truth?
- Am I leading people from my heart?
- Do I stand behind my values and morality?
- How courageous am I?
- How are my team-building abilities?
- Do I dream big enough?
- Do I care about myself in addition to my team?
- Do I focus more on perfection or on doing the best job possible?
- Is what I am doing right now going to leave a legacy?

Reflect upon your passions—are you still passionate about what you've been doing for the last five years? If your answer is no, you might consider moving to a different industry. When you've lost your passion for something, your heart might not be as strongly into leading a team as is best, for both the team and yourself.

Teamwork and Success

At one point in your life you may have heard somebody joke, "There is no 'I' in team...but there's a 'me'!" This common saying is intended to be funny or sarcastic but it may actually have another, more insightful meaning. While it is true that a team consists of a group of people working together, the question is, "Who is leading those people?" That is where *you* are or will be one day—you will find yourself faced with the task of being the team leader. When it's your time to shine, you will be responsible for leading a team to success while fostering important values and ideas and managing conflicts. As a team leader, you will be everyone's "go-to" person, mentor, mediator, and any other role that may come up. When you're in that position, it is up to *you* to build your team and lead it to success.

Stages of Team Development

When you're a leader, you can help develop others into great team players, as your leadership skills will help you be a great team player yourself. Team leaders are responsible for several things when it comes to managing a team. There are five stages of team development, known as the forming, storming, norming, performing and disbanding stages. Each stage is an indicator of progress for a given team. During each stage, it is up to the leader to take action to help move the group through these five stages.

The **forming** stage is usually when the members of a team meet each other for the first time. If they have never worked with each other before, there are usually negative emotions going around, such as fear, distrust, and discomfort. During this stage, it is the responsibility of the team leader to reduce the team's level of discomfort. You can do this by finding common ground on which the team can come together. You can also lead some "ice-breaker" activities to help everyone get to know each other in a non-threatening, non-competitive environment.

The **storming** stage is usually when the team transitions from a regular group of people into the actual team, meaning they start to learn from one another. However, this stage can also cause some conflict. You may find that your team consists of people who have large egos or who can't seem to entertain ideas that differ from their own. As a leader, it is your responsibility to serve as the mediator in this stage. You can encourage everyone to be open about their thoughts and feelings. If any conflicts arise, it is your job to work with the conflicting parties to come up with a solution so that the team can move on to the next stage.

The **norming** stage usually happens once the team gets out of the forming stage. You will know that your team has reached this stage when the team begins to get along and make progress toward the end goal. As a leader, you will probably not have to do much during this stage except work alongside your team and encourage them.

Then there is the **performing** stage. The norming stage will transition into the performing stage as your team begins to seriously make progress. Your team will be in synergy with each other and they will work through any obstacles or challenges that come their way. During this stage, it is up to you to delegate tasks in a strategic fashion. You may also give feedback to team members so that they can improve on their work. Ultimately, you should motivate your team and reward and/or appreciate them during this stage. At this point, you should know your team very well, so you should be able to tell what will work and what won't work with your team members, along with what types of rewards and motivations work best for them.

Finally, the team will move into the **disbanding** stage. This is when the team has achieved the goal and is ready to move on. Sometimes, this means creating new teams with new groups of people. The only risk with this stage is that some team members may be opposed to change, which could heighten the chance of carrying negative emotions into the next team. As a leader, you are responsible for encouraging your team members to embrace change.

Core Values

Throughout the five stages of team development, you will also have to foster and develop **core values**. They are easy to remember because they all start with the letter "C."

The first core value that you must establish as a leader is **communication**. As the leader, you must communicate to your team about their roles and give them feedback as to how they are doing. Without communication, your team will be unable to make progress.

The second core value is **control**. As the leader, it is up to you to have control over your team. You must make sure that the team has control over the work and that you are holding them accountable for their responsibilities.

The third core value is **creativity**. As the leader, it is up to you to encourage and foster creativity. Teams that are creative often have more opportunities and ideas to work with. Creativity can also enhance the communication of the group if everyone shares their ideas.

The fourth core value is **competence**. As the leader, you must make sure that your team is able to complete the tasks given to them. If not, you might need to rethink assignments or retrain team members.

The fifth core value is **collaboration**. Collaboration is a powerful resource when used correctly. As the leader, it is up to you to promote friendly collaboration and to mediate any conflicts that may arise. Collaboration can also go hand-in-hand with creativity.

The sixth core value is **clarity**. As the leader, it is up to you to make sure that your team understands the concept of teamwork as well as the goal they are working towards.

The seventh value is **commitment**. A team that is committed works well together and is in sync with each other. As the leader, it is up to you to encourage commitment as one of the core values of the team.

Finally, to be a great team leader, you must build and practice **good ethics**. As the leader, your team will follow you, so it is crucial to be moral and ethical. This can help strengthen the values of your team and encourage better teamwork. Knowing that they are treated fairly can give your team members a sense of security. It is important to remember that diversity can actually foster more ideas than a team of people who are all very similar. Try to avoid favoritism or singling out any one individual and be sure to treat everyone on the team as equally as possible.

Building Blocks for a Successful Team

Build Good Relationships. Strong, healthy relationships are important for life, especially when it comes to working as a team. Strong relationships between you and your team, as well as among all the team members, can make the difference between success and failure. Teams that foster strong, positive relationships tend to be more productive than teams with clashing, negative relationships. When team members have a strong bond with each other, they are more likely to work above and beyond to produce an amazing end result. The stronger the relationships, the less room there is for negative, uncertain feelings or attitudes.

When it comes to encouraging positive team relationships, you should look back to some of your leadership core values. Be sure to communicate your expectations so that everybody can work together. When team members know their responsibilities, they can work together to be fast and efficient. Don't forget to communicate how important it is to build positive relationships with each other. Communicating with your team can help them build upon their strengths, therefore boosting confidence, which is always an important ingredient for healthy relationships. Encourage the team members to recognize the strengths of each other.

As a leader, you can foster healthy relationships in your team by setting a good example. Set the tone for your project and your team will follow along. As long as you stay consistent, your team will likely get along well, knowing that everyone is working hard toward the same goal. Try to always listen to the concerns of your team members so that you can build a solid foundation of trust. If possible, encourage good relationships outside of the team. Also, be sure to celebrate accomplishments, no matter how large or small. And last, but most important, you should encourage good communication, clarity, commitment and collaboration.

Build Positive Attitudes. A positive attitude can make or break your success. If you go through life with a negative attitude, you will likely see negative outcomes. The same goes for your team. The more positive your team's attitude is toward reaching the end goal, the more productive and successful they are likely to be. A negative attitude will not get you or your team very far.

Encouraging a positive attitude can be easy, especially if you are a naturally optimistic, goals-oriented leader. There are several stages you can follow when promoting positive attitudes. These stages are: civility, respectability, and likeability.

First, as the leader, you must resolve any conflicts that arise during the storming stage. Before you even begin to focus on building a positive attitude, you have to make sure nobody is bumping heads or trying to put the other team players down. This is where your ethics and morale-boosting skills come in. Once you've resolved any conflicts between members, then you can shift your focus to building a team with a great attitude.

Civility is good attitude in its most basic form. With this mindset, you don't have to like or get along with your team members, but you do need to respectfully tolerate them and work together towards the end result as best you can. Civility tries to minimize conflicts or arguments in an attempt to get the project over with as quickly and painlessly as possible. While this attitude is essential in the early stages of your team development, it is important to move your team beyond this stage as soon as possible. The key here is to try and build *strong* relationships, so that the team members not only tolerate each other, but they actually begin to value and like each other.

Respect and valuing others are two attitudes that streamline the productivity of a team. Respect means you value somebody because of certain accomplishments, skills, or personality traits that they possess. For example, you may respect somebody because they have a master's degree, because they are always on time, or because they hold a position of great influence. You can actually encourage specific traits, while honoring individual team members. For example, let's say you have a team member who always meets his deadlines, and no matter what the assignment, you know you can count on him to finish on time. As the leader, you can assign that person to write up the project reports. Not only will you be free from the pressure of doing the reports yourself, but the other team members will notice-and respect -his faithfulness. The example of this single employee can set the standard for the whole team. They may well be challenged to live up to their peer's performance; at the very least, the individual who served as the example should gain some respect from his team-mates.

Assign appropriate tasks to each of your team members, based upon their strengths, abilities, and qualifications. By doing this, you can avoid boring people with work that is no challenge at all, but you also protect team members from feeling overwhelmed by tasks beyond their capabilities. This will help create a positive team identity and each person will feel respected as a valuable member of the group.

Once you've organized your team and assigned them with the tasks that best suit their talents, they will more than likely begin to work well together. Your team will be under control, doing the things they do best, and making progress. Out of respect often comes likeability. When your team is doing tasks they find comfortable and are good at, they are much more likely to open up to each other, get along, and even develop friendships, all of which can help boost the overall spirit of the team.

Foster Communication. Communication is important in teams, otherwise nobody would be able to work together. However, communication is more than just a matter of ensuring your team members talk to each other. Communication is being able to understand each other and convey messages in order to get things done. A team with a high level of communication in their culture is generally much happier and the members work together better. Encourage your team to take note of the way their colleagues communicate; some people are better with nonverbal communication than verbal communication. Understanding this can help your team members feel more safe and respected.

Eliminate Negative Influences From Your Life. Humans are easily influenced by outside sources, which can affect your attitude toward winning, so it is essential to eliminate any negative influences from your life as a part of your leadership strategy. You may think of a negative influence as a person or people in your life but you can also be influenced by other factors, such as what you read, what you watch on television and what you see online. Even if you don't think something you see, hear or read will have a conscious impact on you, it could very well have a subconscious impact.

It is relatively easy to remove negative influences from your life. The first step is to **maintain a positive attitude**. Those who sustain a positive attitude will find it much easier to "tune out" negativity. Usually, when you embrace positivity it is easy to look at things from positive mindset. For example, somebody on your social media friends list may post a negative article, expecting people to feed into it. If you are a positive person, odds are you will just ignore that article and won't be bothered by it.

Here are a few things to remember when practicing positivity:
- Be kind and positive toward anyone in your life who is a complainer. It's usually hard to whine and complain in front of a person who is always so happy and upbeat.

- If you see that somebody around you is starting to gossip or say bad things about a person, simply don't feed into it. Focus your attention on something more important.

- Don't be afraid to constructively criticize someone who is being negative. A person may not realize how negative he or she is being. Sometimes it helps to have an outside source fill you in on how you sound, because it is hard to see your own weaknesses.

The second step is to plan to **avoid negative influences from the media.** Media outlets love to publish negative stories because they often generate a large response from their audience. However, you can easily avoid these outlets and stick to ones that are more unbiased. A good way to start is to do some research and find out which news outlets in your area publish unbiased stories. If you have friends on your social media accounts who often post negative things, you can easily hide them from your feed without unfriending them. In addition, try to focus on local newspapers, since they tend to post more positive stories than their national counterparts.

The third step to removing negativity from your life is to **maintain positive relationships**. The people you associate with every day are often major influences on you, so one of your goals should be to limit your interaction to positive company.

Can you think of any friends who are negative influences? Those friends are the kind who belittle your goals and ideas, saying things like "Oh that's unrealistic" or "I think that's a waste of time." If any friends come immediately to mind, you may want to rethink your friendship with them. You don't necessarily need to break it off entirely, but you should definitely pay attention to how much time you spend with that person and take steps to dilute their negative influence.

A good way to spot others who are positive is to look at their habits. Positive people often make it a <u>habit</u> to eat right, exercise and otherwise take care of their bodies. Those who are more apt to lie around and not take care of themselves are usually the people who tend to be more negative.

Chapter 7: Creativity, Organization and Success

Creativity has been a hot social topic during the past couple of decades. You have probably heard people talking about it in several contexts. You've probably heard others say that the children of today aren't creative anymore. Maybe you've heard someone opine that the future of this world depends upon our creativity. Many people believe that parents and teachers should value it more and encourage it more often. Well, what exactly is creativity, and why is it so important?

The general definition of creativity is to create or improve upon something with an original idea. Creativity is what has generated many of your favorite movies, books, songs, TV shows, paintings, and sculptures. Creativity is also what helps create innovative new products and unique, successful businesses. It also plays a part in science, economics, cognitive psychology and many other fields and disciplines. Creativity is intangible; it can be spread and shared throughout the world. It is what keeps the world evolving. Some would say that creativity is what keeps life fun. Without creativity, the world would be lacking many incredible breakthroughs that have transformed our lives for the better in so many ways.

The Benefits of Creativity

- **Creativity Can Help You Solve Problems Better.** When you have mastered the art of being able to use your creative thinking skills, it can in turn improve your ability to become a better problem solver. There is no instructional guide to creation, so creativity can help your brain get in a better habit of thinking independently and confidently.

- **Creativity Helps You Get Involved and Meet Others.** When you create something and you want to share it with the world (or maybe just your local community, for starters), you have the opportunity to connect with others who share your ideals. Your creation gives you the opportunity to exchange feedback with other creators. Finally, you stand a higher chance of helping others, especially if your creation is useful and practical. Even if you just write a small book, it could help others escape from their own realities or help them solve some important problems.

- **Creativity Can Help You Save Money.** You've probably never heard of this one before, but it's true. Research shows that when you're better able to express yourself, your chances of making impulse purchases can dramatically decrease. As an added benefit, creating something can help you feel more fulfilled, unlike making an impulse buy. So, by being creative, you can save money and feel great about yourself at the same time.

- **Creativity Can Help You Establish Self-Awareness.** Being creative can help you gain a better and more fulfilling sense of self-awareness. When you create, you tend to explore your thoughts and beliefs more deeply. This can lead you to better understand yourself, your habits, your needs, and your wants. In turn, this can also help you express yourself better.

- **Creativity Grants You Freedom.** When you create something of your own, you're in charge. Unlike your job, where you've probably got to follow a set of rules and standards, anything is possible when you create, hence giving you a sense of freedom. There is no right or wrong way to create something of your own. This can help you get into the habit of risk-taking and opportunity-grabbing.

- **Creativity Can Keep You Healthy.** Creativity can help you improve your physical and mental health. When you create something, you tend to become happier and more resilient. You may also feel a reduction in anxiety. Creativity can also help combat mental stress. Research has shown that people who report being stressed out tend to have weight issues, higher glucose levels, more upper respiratory problems and a higher chance of developing heart disease. By being creative, you can help yourself become less stressed out and anxious, therefore limiting your chances of developing some physical problems.

- **Creativity Can Help You Stay On Track In Life.** Creativity also tends to give you an idea of your life's purpose. Without it, you may feel emptier inside. When you're feeling empty inside, your chances of trying to fill the void with fake friends, materialism, medication, alcohol and drugs highly increases.

Creative Habits

Believe in Your Idea. People who come up with new ideas often feel self-conscious about them or are afraid of being judged. When that happens, their creativity tends to crash. To be able to create something to your best ability, you should **believe** in yourself and in your idea. One good way to reinforce your belief in yourself and your ideas is to make a positive declaration. Stand in front of a mirror, put your hand over your heart, and say, "I can and I will create this."

Pay Attention to Details. When you pay attention to details, you face a higher chance of living in the present moment. When you're living in the present, your world tends to become more alive and interactive, which can be very helpful in becoming creative. When you begin to notice small details about things, you tend to feel more inspired and thoughtful. By paying attention to details, you can also get into the mindset of looking at things from a different angle, which can also be helpful in stimulating your creativity.

Set Restrictions. Setting restrictions for yourself is a way to create a challenge, which can inspire you to think of creative ways around the obstacle. This is how Dr. Seuss ended up writing the bestseller *Green Eggs and Ham*. A friend had bet him that he couldn't write a story within a specific word-count. If you're a writer, challenge yourself to write a five-hundred-word story if you're used to writing two-thousand-word stories. If you're an artist, challenge yourself to draw something in thirty minutes instead of an hour. Whatever type of project you're working on or whatever field you're working in, set a restriction for yourself and see how it affects your creative thinking.

Organization and Success

We've all dealt with the perils of disorganization. You wake up late, slip on piles of unwashed clothes on the way to the shower, scramble to stuff an unhealthy breakfast in your mouth, and still manage to be late for work. Your brain feels cluttered, and it affects not only your mood but the moods of those around you. You may feel like you are always giving excuses for one mishap after another due to the disorganization problems that have piled up.

Organization affects many more parts of your life than you may assume. It can seem like a difficult beast to tackle, but if you're able to take a brief step back, decide what's most important to you in your life, and make conscious decisions every day to make these a priority; then you're well on your way to being far more organized and living much more happily and efficiently.

Keeping Your Home Organized

- Avoid dust with weekly cleanings, keeping you and your loved ones happy and sniffle free.

- Keep inventory of your beauty products and put together a morning and evening routine.

- Take some time once a week to plan your grocery shopping and meals for the week. Shop smart, and never while hungry.

- Choose surroundings that soothe and empower you. Avoid jarring patterns.

Bottom line; make the time in your schedule to plan for an organized home. If you make the time, sit down, and make a plan, you're already on your way to an organized home. If you still find that you are overwhelmed with things, then organize your closets and sell off everything that you don't need. You may be shocked at just how good you can feel when you give away, throw away, or sell all that extra stuff that you never use anymore! Check out this YouTube video to help get yourself motivated and ready for an organized and clutter free life: How To Become A Minimalist by Danny Dover.

Organizing Your Digital Life for Success

- **Keep Each Project's Contents in One Place.** If you're working on a multimedia project—photos, spreadsheets, word documents etc.—have have them all organized in their own special place on your computer. One good idea is to save each media type in one general or *master* folder so that it is much easier to navigate through everything quickly and easily. This can save you time bouncing around your computer, trying to track down what you need.

- **Back up Regularly.** It can't be said enough, every piece of digital content you've ever created can be gone in a second. Put together a regular backup routine, copying all files to an external hard drive or cloud based software. I like to group all my files in one place under "personal" and "business." I can then easily highlight these areas and then save them to an external hard drive quite easily.

- **Use Tags to Organize and Find Your Photos.** After you move your photos to your computer from your camera or phone, take a few minutes to organize them, using tags. Several tools that can help with this include QNAP's Photo Station and Google Picasa. Some can even recognize faces, which speeds up the process further. Once your photos are tagged, you can search for them on your computer just like any other file type. Otherwise, you can organize pictures using folders. I personally have folders for my favorite pictures, I have one folder for the pictures I use most often, and the rest I store in folders organized by date. There are a variety of great programs that will allow you to organize your photo collection very easily.

- **OneNote or EverNote.** I can't recommend getting a program like OneNote or EverNote enough! A friend told me about OneNote sixteen months ago and I ignored her advice for about four months. I finally got around to looking into it and all I can say is: **"WOW!"** This program has been life changing. I have been using it for the past year and I have my life set up like a peak performance mastermind genius! If used properly, you can organize so much there! Some of the incredible features of OneNote is that it automatically saves things instantly, you can put links to websites and YouTube videos in there, you can easily create a digital journal just by organizing entries according to month, you can have a whole section dedicated to your personal life and a another section dedicated to business, then further divide those groups into all the different aspects that you want super quick and easy access to. I put everything on OneNote and then make sure the backup of the file is in an easy-to-access folder which can then be readily backed up online or on an external hard drive. I would highly recommend a program like this because it allows you to easily organize almost every aspect of your digital life.

Top 10 Tips for Organization

1. **Make the time.** Set aside some time each week to decompress and make your organizational plan for the days ahead. Taking advantage of this time will help you be fully equipped and prepared for the challenges of the week ahead and you'll go into Monday with a clear, focused mind.

2. **List it.** Lists (digital or hand written) will be your mapping tool to full organization. Keep track of errands, which need to be run, groceries that need to be purchased, calls to be returned, and other to-dos that need to be taken care of. Keep these lists in an easily accessible area of your phone, computer, or notebook.

3. **Prep your meals.** Chop, can and store all ingredients for your lunches in the week to come. Freeze any ingredients you can in airtight containers and plastic bags so that they last longer. Buy ingredients in bulk whenever you can and use perishables in a timely manner before they go bad.

4. **Clean your house regularly.** A clean and tidy house is inviting; it will encourage you to spend more time at home, instead of spending money going out. Keeping your house neat and clean will also encourage you to appreciate it more.

5. **Do a digital cleanup.** Get rid of excess documents, emails, photos, and music to open up space on your computer. Organize the files you hold on to in specific folders that are easily accessible. Make sure that all assets are labeled correctly and are easy to track down.

6. **Don't spread yourself too thin.** You have twenty-four hours in your day, seven days in your week. Use these hours to your advantage. Sometimes this will mean saying no to happy hours or a friend's request to hang out. You know what your goals and dreams are and what it will take for you to be successful. Success almost never comes easily, but those who are the most disciplined and hardest working are usually the ones smiling with the trophy in their hand at the end.

7. **Breathe.** Everything is fixable. Nothing is so urgent that you can't stop and think things through. Remember to stop and think of possible responses before you choose to act.

Some of these suggestions will be more applicable to your life than others. Still struggling with getting started? Pick your top three suggestions to tackle in the coming weeks. Start with just one and try to integrate it into your daily life. Once you've gotten the hang of it, add another top-ten tip to your routine. Don't beat yourself up if you have off days, these are all part of the process. Over time you'll appreciate how much better you feel with these practices woven into your life. I can tell you that I personally have almost every area of my life expertly organized; I have found it truly amazing how much more efficient, happy and productive you truly can be when everything is in its proper place!

Chapter 8: Finances and Success

Can you think of any other material object that causes more problems in peoples' lives than money? If money is in short supply, it can often lead to mental stress, personal problems, and a slew of other negative consequences. Mental stress from lack of money can tire you out, wear you down, and make you physically sick. It can take away from your best performances and it can determine whether you keep a job, maintain a relationship, or have a happy life. Some people let their money problems go unresolved for so long that they end up entirely consuming everything they have. Unresolved money problems can come back to haunt you in the future, too. They can ruin your credit score and make it harder for you to take out loans and mortgages. Once your credit has gone bad, then it is even more expensive for you to get around in daily life!

When you're in control of your finances, you won't have to worry about living "paycheck to paycheck", as many people do today. Best of all, you won't have to live on such a tight budget. By taking charge of your money, by being proactive instead of reactive, you will find you may have more money to do leisurely things or enjoy some of the "extras" you want, such as nice dinners out or that new jacket you've been eying at the mall. You can even save up enough money to make a major life purchase, such as a house or a sports car. When you have enough money, you won't be afraid to look at your monthly bank statements and you'll feel great, knowing that you've mastered one of the most difficult and important areas of your life!

In this chapter, you will discover how to better manage your money and finances to ensure that you do not get consumed by money problems. The less you have to worry about your money and finances, the more time and resources you can put toward becoming successful.

Build a Savings Account

The best way to manage your money is to keep it in a bank account. The two most common types of checking accounts that most people have are checking and savings accounts. By keeping money in a checking account, you can gain easy access to your spending money by writing out a check or swiping a debit card. A savings account works differently. Many people put money into a savings account for the purposes of, obviously, saving. You might open a savings account to save money for emergencies or to spend later. Money that you put into a savings account can earn interest over a period of time. Best of all, you don't need a large amount of money to start a savings account. Depending on your bank, you might only need as little as $25 to begin. Some banks charge a low monthly fee or offer savings accounts for free based on maintaining a certain balance, and interest rates vary from bank to bank. Always shop around before deciding on a bank for your savings account. You should generally be able get one for free.

There are many benefits to opening a savings account. First and foremost, your chances of spending money held in a savings account are much lower than if your money was in a checking account. Secondly, your money is safe in a savings account. If your house were ever to get burglarized, or if a tornado ripped through your neighborhood and swept your house away, your money would still be safe and sound in the bank. Money in a savings account is also safe because it is insured by the FDIC if you live in the USA. This means, if your bank were to close, you wouldn't lose your money. Finally, many people open savings accounts to accrue interest. That occurs when your bank *pays* you money for the privilege of lending your money to others. When that happens, your bank will usually pay you interest every month.

Basic savings accounts, which usually only require small fees to get started, only earn a small amount of interest each month. A market money account will gain a higher amount of interest, but often comes with limitations. For example, you need a lot of money to put into it and you are restricted in the number of withdrawals you can make in a month.

Once you've opened a savings account, your bank will give you a log where you can track your money. You can also track your deposits, withdrawals, fees, and interest gains by reading your monthly statements. To learn more about the different types of savings accounts that your bank may offer, check out this video, Money Management: Types of Savings Accounts by eHowFinance.

Saving vs. Paying Off Debt

Most expert financial advisers agree that you should save between 10 and 20% of your income. However, the actual rate of savings for the majority of the United States is only 4.2%. Why is that? It's because many U.S. citizens are piled up to their necks in debt. The most common type of debt is credit card debt. Many people find themselves in bad credit card debt because credit cards easily bring feelings of instant gratification. That brings many people to the question of, "Should I focus on saving or on paying off my debt?" While it is important to save, paying off high-interest debts as fast as you can, should be your first priority.

As always, here is an example that may help you understand this better: let's pretend that you have a $10,000 credit card debt with a 15% interest rate. The bank requires a minimum payment of 1% of the principal balance plus interest. That means your minimum payment per month is $225. Breaking it down even further, you would see that $100 of your payment goes toward your principal and the other $125 goes straight to the bank to pay for interest. If you were to continue paying off that debt using the monthly minimum amount, it would take you nearly thirty years to pay it *and* it would cost you an additional $12,000 just in interest!

Let's look at a different scenario: say, now you can pay $400 a month toward that debt. You'd be able to pay off your debt in just two years and you would save $10,000 in interest, compared to what you'd normally pay over five years. Instead of losing all of your money to the bank, you'd still have it, only in a savings account.

The greatest benefit that comes with paying off your debt is that you will have a guaranteed rate of return on your money. You'll be out of debt sooner than you know and you won't have to pay so much in interest. However, you should save a small amount of money before you start paying off your debts, just in case an emergency arises.

Wiring Your Brain for Financial Success

Review Your Emotions. Your emotions can have a huge influence on how you view money. As many experts have theorized, your thoughts lead to feelings, your feelings lead to actions, and your actions lead to results. The key is to understand what is driving your feelings, as your feelings are what start the chain of results. Your emotions toward money can strongly influence how you end up handling it. Think about how money was viewed in your household while you were growing up— did you ever hear your parents or guardians say things such as, "money is the root of all evil" or "rich people are stingy and greedy; they aren't like us?" If you grew up hearing those things in person or on TV, then there is a good chance you are letting your emotions take charge of your finances as an adult. Luckily, there are ways to change your emotions toward money.

Review Your Financial Habits. Your habits are the second biggest factor in influencing how you manage your money. Habits are things that you do automatically, so if you have bad financial habits, chances are your money management is poor. For example, if you always have to buy a treat when you go to the store, you'll want to break that habit to avoid spending more money than you ought, especially if you could get a better deal online or at another store. If you're used to living off other people, you'll definitely want to break this habit. Someday you just might wind up on your own, with no idea how to handle money, if you don't develop healthy financial habits now.

Review Your Specific Beliefs About Money. Finally, you must dig deep and grasp the roots of what is causing your **most specific, emotional belief** about money. When you were little, what do remember experiencing that concerned money? Many people grow up believing false assumptions, such as "men are the breadwinners," or "women are meant to stay home and take care of the house," or "money is what makes people get divorced," etc. Whatever assumptions and specific emotional memories you have of money can seriously influence the way you handle it.

Wire Your Brain Continuously. Once you have consciously made the decision to eradicate any nonproductive beliefs about money, the next step is to wire your brain to start handling money better. Think about what you're making now and how you're spending it. Can you do better? Are you struggling to pay your bills? Answering all of these questions is very important to properly reprogram your brain to handle money. Once you have answered these questions, it's time to start using positive affirmations to combat your old negative thinking and behavior. You also want to program your brain for financial abundance. You can visualize money coming to you in all sorts of different ways; you can try to think of one hundred dollar bills as one dollar bills to help program your brain for financial abundance. I would also highly recommend Hypnosis for those who are serious about programming their brain for financial success. My favorite source for great audios is Hypnosis Downloads. I personally use and can highly recommend "The Millionaire Mindset" bundle package or you can try: "Overcome Fear of Money."

Chapter 9: Ultimate Success Strategies

Congratulations, you've made it this far! Hopefully by now you are much more familiar with the core principles of success and you have some ideas on how to rework your life according to them. But before you do that, this chapter will help you discover even more success strategies that you can use to customize your own plan. Let's take a look, starting with the most important strategy...

Define Success

It is nearly impossible to create success without first defining it. Your definition of success could be the complete opposite of your friends', your parents', your siblings' or anyone else's in the world; to be successful you need to know what it means to *you*. As with goal-setting, your definition of success should be crystal clear and specific. The more clear and specific your definition of success, the easier it is to visualize; by now you know all about the power of visualization and how you can use it can help yourself.

What does success mean to you? For many, the definition of success revolves around a variety of cultural beliefs. Many Americans regard success from a monetary viewpoint. You probably know somebody who communicates his success through his car, home, and/or clothes. Other cultures tend to view success from a family-based standpoint, an effectiveness viewpoint, a pleasure viewpoint, or whether their success creates a balance in life. Each person's perspective on success will be different; it may not necessarily depend on your culture or where you are from. I know people who feel successful when they are making progress in their life; I also know people who feel successful when they genuinely love what they're doing. What is *your* definition of success?

A good way to create your definition of success is to consider your core values. If you value family over all else, then your definition of success may mean having a balance between work and personal time. If you value human rights and equality, your definition of success may equate to effectiveness in supporting these. Creating your own definition may not happen overnight—in fact, it could take days, weeks, or months. Defining success often becomes a personal journey. It may take you some trial and error, mistakes, and some high points and low points, until you figure out what success means to you.

Set Goals and Plan for Success

I've touched upon this throughout the book already, but I cannot emphasize too strongly how important it is to set goals and actually plan out your success. Too many people just assume that success will come to them naturally, without having to do much.

I know somebody who is really intelligent and did very well in school. One of her first dreams was to make it to Hollywood and become a movie director. She thought to herself, "Well I'm really smart and I do great at achieving things in school so I'll have no problem becoming a famous director." Instead of pursuing special high schools and colleges with directing programs and taking initiative to meet other people in the field, my friend goofed off throughout those years without having a plan at all and needless to say, she has not made it to Hollywood.

In general, having a plan helps you stay on track with your goals, while not having a plan allows you to wander and lose focus. In this case, if my friend had planned to research schools and programs that focused on direction and media as well as setting some goals to seek out mentors through networking, she might have actually gotten somewhere.

Find the Strength to Leave Your Comfort Zone

Staying in your comfort zone can be, well, comforting. However, remaining in this place can hold you back from experiencing the best open doors. If you never leave your comfort zone, you risk living a mediocre life, in which you never quite reach the top and miss out on opportunities that you deserve. People like this are often fearful, lazy, or simply lacking in willpower to face hard work. Never accept the "easy way out." If you avoid risks and new experiences, you will more than likely miss out on important chances for personal growth and development; these can be key components to achieving success. Pain may be awful but it's often a very good teacher. If you have ever touched a hot stove, then you probably realize how powerful a teacher pain can be.

I know that leaving your comfort zone can be scary. Luckily, you can do some things to gradually build up your confidence and eventually prepare yourself to leap boundaries. It can be as simple as taking a cold shower in the morning or going "cold turkey" on social media or some other type of electronic device you rely on every day. Get into the habit of striking up conversations with strangers. Say yes when you would normally say no (as long as you're not agreeing to do something illegal or harmful to your health). Gradually build up your confidence by taking greater and greater risks until you feel able to tackle major challenges to your comfort zone.

There are incentives to leaving your comfort zone, which you may find very motivating. You may find your life more productive; you may find it ten times easier to adjust to changes than ever before. You may also find it easier to flex your creativity. All of these incentives may help you land a new job and/or make more money. Breaking out of your comfort zone can help you push your boundaries and achieve things you never thought possible.

Avoid Popularity and Seek Respect

Respect and popularity are two different things that often collide with each other. If somebody is popular, the majority may like him but if he does not stay consistent with his word or values, he is not likely to have any respect. When people respect you, popularity often comes as a byproduct. Seek respect first and let the popularity take care of itself.

Model Yourself after Others but Remain Innovative

Modeling your success after another successful person or business is a really good strategy. After all, you have to start somewhere; finding a role model or mentor is the perfect starting point. You can model yourself after a person you know, a business you read about in a book or a combination of factors. For businesses, many states have SCORE chapters, an organization run by former businesspeople that is dedicated to help rising entrepreneurs get started. I've personally found that reading books about successful people and ventures can help you model yourself for success.

The potential problem of modeling is the chance of imitating the personality and not the principles that led to success. Your goal is not to copy another person or business precisely, but to use your model as a guide. For example, you may choose to model yourself after your boss, a self-disciplined, focused person who gets good results but only by scaring his employees into working hard. You could model his ability to focus and his self-discipline, but you may want to think of a better way to motivate employees than scaring them.

Be yourself and be innovative. Never lose sight of who you are or what you and/or your business stand for. Work your knowledge like your muscles—build on what you already know and sharpen it to become an expert. Don't fall into the trap of trying to be the best at everything. Pick one area of expertise that you're really good at and use that as your starting point. Explore it deeply and ask questions to see what new, innovative ideas you can pull out of it.

Do the Unspoken

Take risks and do what most people won't. This is a part of being innovative. If you don't dare to do something different, you risk becoming trapped in your comfort zone. Remember, if you won't risk change, then you probably won't make a difference. A good way to prevent yourself from falling into the ineffective majority is to figure out what most people fail to do. For example, many new businesses fail within the first year. If you can figure out what it takes to overcome that first year then you are at an advantage. Many people refuse to question their deeply-rooted beliefs. If you dare to do that, you may find yourself pleasantly surprised with fresh, innovative ideas. To find success in your life, figure out what those around you are afraid to do or cannot do, then push yourself to overcome your own resistance.

Keep a Journal of Your Progress

Keeping a journal of your progress is a great strategy for success. Research shows that when you write down your goals you are more likely to achieve them. Not only should you write down your goals, but you should also write down your ideas, fears, thoughts, feelings, and your progress. I personally like to write whenever I make a mistake. I write about what I did, how I did it wrong and how I can fix my mistakes for next time and I've found that helpful. I also personally favor journaling because I like to go back and read about my progress. I find it very inspirational and fun to see how far I've come along and when I see that, it makes me want to be even better.

Don't Isolate Yourself

All too often, people get caught up trying to work so hard toward success that they end up spending too much time by themselves. While it is important to focus on your work alone it is equally important to feed your social life. The best way to take advantage of your social life is to reach out to other people in your profession. You can go to networking events or join an online community with the types of people who are likely to help you succeed. These people can give you better, more tailored advice; they can mentor you, give you pep talks, and share their own success stories. Taking a break from your work is also important; you should avoid burning yourself out, which can make you less likely to succeed.

Start Small but Dream Big

Starting off small is important for all success. You cannot become successful at anything overnight. Many successful endeavors have been a result of baby steps. This is similar to goal-setting, in which you set several short-term goals in order to help you reach your overall long-term goal. However, you should not mistake starting off small for staying small. Don't forget to create powerful visualizations of ultimate success. Never settle for where you are in the present. Always seek out a bigger, better opportunity. Always remember that there are limitless options and possibilities at your fingertips.

Follow the 80/20 Rule

The 80/20 Rule states that 80% of your results come from 20% of your work. In other words, 20% of what you do accounts for the majority of what goes on in your life. You can apply the 80/20 rule to almost any aspect of your life: finances, business, health, leadership, etc. For the 80/20 Rule to work efficiently for you, you'll have to figure out your most important 20%. You will have to narrow down what activities and actions will get you the results you're looking for. For example, you may be looking to improve your health and diet so you may need to focus your 20% on managing your diet or maybe you need to focus on.

Here are some more questions to ask yourself, just to give you an idea of how this rule works:

- What 20% of my time generates 80% of my happiness?

- What 20% of my friends/family generates 80% of my self-esteem?

- What 20% of food do I eat 80% of the time?

- What 20% of exercise do I do that makes me feel great 80% of the time?

- What 20% of activities I do with my spouse will generate 80% of our best times?

Don't be afraid to ask these questions backwards so you know how to manage your life accordingly. For example, figure out the 80% of friends/family who only account for 20% of your self-esteem and spend less time with them.

In terms of business and work, it is easy to apply the 80/20 Rule if you're doing something that you're passionate about. Some people have specific ideas about what their passion is and other people need to discover it through trial and error. A big part of using the 80/20 Rule is to manage your time effectively. Obviously you should prioritize the most important 20% of your tasks that will get you the most important 80% of your results and put your other tasks on the back burner. Another good way to multiply your results is to develop your skills to the point where you can get the same things done in less time.

Never Stop Learning

I once received a really good piece of advice from one of my mentors: Never say "I knew that." Even if you are an expert on something, there is always room to learn something new or look at something in a different way. For example, a lot of businesses find success due to rapidly changing trends now-a-days; with trends, you always have to stay on top to stay ahead. These days, you don't have to go to school or sit in a classroom to learn. My favorite way of learning is to read books, both hardcover and not. There is also an abundance of free resources on the internet that you can use to your advantage. Don't forget about workshops, seminars, lectures, etc.

Master the Art of Selling

Though you may not hold a career as a salesperson, I think knowing how to be a seller is paramount to success. When it comes down to it, you're going to have to sell yourself no matter what industry you work in or what you do in life. For example, I write books but writing books alone doesn't make me money. I have to oversee the sales and marketing of these books. So I may be an author but to be a successful author I have to also be a successful salesperson. Sales skills are important for persuading others to listen to/try out your ideas, essential for getting a job, and important to building a strong list of friends and acquaintances; they even come in handy with your personal life. A teenager might find it helpful to sell an idea to her parents and persuade them to say "yes." A guy might try to sell himself to a girl for a chance to take her out on a date.

In terms of business, here are some of the top sales tips I have to help you get started:

Challenge Everyone's Comfort Level

As a person who works in sales or whose job it is to generate sales, you already know how tricky it can be to accomplish your sales goals sometimes. Have you ever thought about just *why* sales can be so tricky? The answer is really simple—people become comfortable and happy with what they already have. Many of those working in sales believe the problem is that people are unwilling to pay money for things they don't need, but that couldn't be farther from the truth! In fact, some people are willing to pay top dollar for the best of the best, in terms of something that can help them get to where they want to be.

The real problem is one for you to solve. The best way to generate sales is to challenge the status quo of your clients. Your clients are happy with what they have, hence the reason they haven't come running to you. Your job is to challenge this mindset, get into your clients' heads, and start piquing their interest.

The first step is to find out what your client *wants*... not what he or she needs, but what he or she really *wants*. Usually the number one mistake people in sales are taught is to go after what a client needs. A client who needs something will go out and get it; it won't matter where it's from. You wake up and your teeth are feeling nasty—you *need* toothpaste—it won't matter if it's Crest, Aim or some generic brand. You haven't eaten all day and you're hungry—you need to eat—and you'll probably go for whatever you can get. It doesn't matter whether it's a home-cooked meal, McDonalds, or a frozen dinner; they will take whatever is the closest and most convenient. Even when it comes down to love, people need to feel love and affection and sometimes they will look for it anywhere. You may be thinking, "If I were in these scenarios, I wouldn't go for the first thing I could get to fulfill my needs, I would go for brand x or brand y." That is the key here—people have needs and they want to fulfil them with what they *prefer*. That's where the loophole exists. You need to brush your teeth but maybe there is a certain brand you prefer because of the ingredients or anti-cavity properties; you need to eat, but maybe you prefer something healthy because it is aligned with your health values, etc.

Pique Their Interest and Let Them "Discover" Something

Many people think of things such as outer space or animal science when it comes to the word "discovery." Who makes discoveries every day? You may think it is just scientists or researchers. However, for the no-name consumer, a discovery can be a breath of fresh air from the boredom of everyday life. When a consumer discovers something about a product or service, he is more likely to tell others about it, lending your company some free word-of-mouth marketing. When a person discovers something, it helps her feel smarter, which in turn can boost her self-esteem. Discoveries, for a consumer, often come in the form of a new idea or a new and improved way to get things done. If your product or service falls into the category of something that is helpful to your consumer and/or it can benefit their life, this can be a good marketing tool. Use keywords that promote a possible improvement in the consumer's life. "New" is a keyword that often works well and piques interest. Be sure to tailor your sales pitch in a way that lets the customer know what is new or interesting about your product or service.

Find out What's Going On in a Prospect's Life

When you ask the right kind of questions to your prospective client it opens up an opportunity for you to find additional selling points. An easy and effective way to do this is to find out what's going on in your client's personal life. Usually life events such as a move, a marriage, a divorce, a graduation, or a promotion can be used as a hot spot for upselling or getting your client to buy an additional product or service. For example, let's pretend that you work in an electronics store and some of your bonus pay comes from commissions. You have a customer come in looking to buy a new laptop. After asking the right questions, maybe in this case "What's caused you to need a new laptop," you learn that this customer is actually an upcoming freshman in college. You can now take this information and work with it…maybe by showing them the TVs you have on display or the graphing calculators or anything else that a freshman in college may need. More often than not, that customer will probably end up buying something in addition to what he or she originally came in for, especially if they think it will help them or view it as an upgrade.

Develop Your Communication Skills

Communication skills, verbal and nonverbal, are also paramount to success. The better your communication skills, the more likely you are to be successful. Modern technology has done everything but encourage intrapersonal skills. With text messaging, social media and email it is easier than ever to hide behind a screen and lose your ability to communicate in person. Mastering verbal communication can help you build rapport with others, which often leads to golden opportunities. Just your body language alone can make or break a deal; knowing how to use it to your advantage can push you ahead. Making a strong first impression on others is important; good communication skills can ensure you do just that. If you're shy or introverted, you can easily build your communication skills. A good place to start is in front of a mirror; dress nicely and take good care of yourself, because that alone can boost your confidence, which can directly affect how well you communicate with others.

Chapter 10: Inspirational Quotes

This chapter simply contains a broad selection of inspirational and motivational quotes about success. I highly suggest reading through this chapter, picking out some of your favorites, and referring to them every day. This can help you keep striving toward success. You can write these quotes down and keep them in your workspace, on your phone, or any other place where your eyes will look frequently.

"Give me a stock clerk with a goal and I'll give you a man who will make history. Give me a man with no goals and I'll give you a stock clerk" – James Cash Penny

"A goal is a dream with a deadline" – Napoleon Hill

"The person who gets the farthest is generally the one who is willing to do and dare. The sure-thing boat never gets far from shore" – Dale Carnegie

"The state of your life is nothing more than a reflection of your state of mind" – Wayne Dyer

"Most successful men have not achieved their distinction by having some new talent or opportunity presented to them. They have developed the opportunity that was at hand" – Bruce Barton

"Shoot for the moon. Even if you miss, you'll land among the stars" – Les Brown

"Would you like me to give you a formula for success? It's quite simple, really. Double your rate of failure. You are thinking of failure as the enemy of success. But it isn't at all. You can be discouraged by failure or you can learn from it, so go ahead and make mistakes. Make all you can. Because remember that's where you will find success" – Thomas J. Watson

"Fix your eyes on perfection and you make almost everything speed towards it" – William Ellery Channing

"The successful always has a number of projects planned, to which he looks forward. Anyone of them could change the course of his life overnight" – Mark Caine

"A winner is someone who recognizes his God given talents, works his tail off to develop them into skills, and uses these skills to accomplish his goals" – Larry Bird

"There are three ingredients in the good life: learning, earning and yearning" – Christopher Morley

"If you take responsibility for yourself you will develop a hunger to accomplish your dreams" – Les Brown

"When a man feels throbbing within him the power to do what he undertakes as well as it can possibly be done, this is happiness, this is success" – Orison Swett Marden

"A good plan today is better than a great plan tomorrow" – George S. Patton

"What distinguishes us one from another is our dreams…and what we do to make them come about" – Joseph Epstein

"The great successful men of the world have used their imagination. They think ahead and create their mental picture in all its details, filling in here, adding a little there, altering this a bit and that a bit, but steadily building - steadily building" – Robert Collier

"Celebrate any progress. Don't wait to get perfect" – Ann McGee Cooper

"If you do what you've always done, you'll get what you've always gotten" – Anthony Robbins

"The difference between a successful person and others is not a lack of strength, not a lack of knowledge, but rather in a lack of will" - Vincent T. Lombardi

"What the mind can conceive and believe, it can achieve" – Napoleon Hill

"Every great human achievement is preceded by extended periods of dedicated, concentrated effort" – Brain Tracy

"Coming together is a beginning; keeping together is a progress; working together is success" – Henry Ford

"Use the losses and failures of the past as a reason for action, not inaction" – Charles J. Givens

"The world of achievement has always belonged to the optimist" – J. Harold Wilkins

"Success is not final, failure is not fatal: it is the courage to continue that counts" – Winston Churchill

"Each one of us has a fire in our heart for something. It's our goal in life to find it and keep it lit" – Mary Lou Retton

"To succeed in life, you need two things: ignorance and confidence" – Mark Twain

"If you have built castles in the air, your work need not be lost; that is where they should be. Now put the foundations under them" – Henry David Thoreau

"A successful man is one who can lay a firm foundation with the bricks others have thrown at him" – David Brinkley

"The discipline you learn and character you build from setting and achieving a goal can be more valuable than the achievement of the goal itself" – Bo Bennett

"I've failed over and over and over again in my life and that is why I succeed" – Michael Jordan

"Success is never final and failure never fatal. It's courage that counts" – George F. Tiltonood

"Put your future in good hands. Your own" – Mark Victor Hansen

"Success depends upon previous preparation, and without such preparation there is sure to be failure" – Confucius

"The key is not to prioritize what's on your schedule, but to schedule your priorities" – Stephen R. Covey

"Those who do not create the future they want must endure the future they get" – Draper L. Kaufman, Jr.

"Success is to be measured not so much by the position that one has reached in life as by the obstacles which he has overcome" – Booker T. Washington

"Don't let anyone tell you that you can't do it. You can. It's up to you. Decide to do it and follow through" – Porter Freeman

"Action is the foundational key to all success" – Pablo Picasso

"Great minds have purposes, others have wishes" – Washington Irving

"I've always made a total effort, even when the odds seemed entirely against me. I never quit trying; I never felt that I didn't have a chance to win" – Arnold Palmer

"The most important single ingredient in the formula of success is knowing how to get along with people" – Theodore Roosevelt

"When your values are clear to you, making decisions becomes easier" – Roy Disney

"A great pleasure in life is doing what people say you cannot do" – Walter Bagehot

"If you have no critics you'll likely have no success" – Malcolm X

"The more you listen to the voice within you, the better you will hear what is sounding outside" – Dag Hammarskjold

"When you cannot make up your mind which of two evenly balanced courses of action you should take, choose the bolder" – W.J. Slim

"Any time you're tempted to say, "Impossible", add an apostrophe and a space, and say, "I'm possible"" - Al Secunda

"If you don't quit, and don't cheat, and don't run home when trouble arrives, you can only win" – Shelley Long

"If you don't risk anything, you risk even more" – Erica Jong

"Fear paralyzes; curiosity empowers. Be more interested than afraid" – Patricia Alexander

"Questions focus our thinking. Ask empowering questions like, what's good about this? What's not perfect about it yet? What am I going to do next time? How can I do this and have fun doing it?" – Charles Connolly

"A problem is a chance to do your best" – Duke Ellington

"Every really new idea looks crazy at first" – Abraham Maslow

"Mistakes are merely steps up the ladder" – Paul J. Meyer

"Knowledge is power. The more knowledge, expertise, and connections you have, the easier it is for you to make a profit at the game of your choice" – Stuart Wilde

"Remember: if you're not experiencing failure, you're not working hard enough" – Jeffery J. Mayer

"He that is good with a hammer tends to think everything is a nail" – Abraham Maslow

"Time is our most valuable asset, yet we tend to waste it, kill it, and spend it rather than invest it" – Jim Rohn

"If passion drives you, let reason hold the reigns" – Benjamin Franklin

"Your attitude, not your aptitude, will determine your altitude" – Zig Ziglar

"Luck is what happens when preparation meets opportunity" – Elmer Letterman

"Men may doubt what you say, but they will believe what you do" – Lewis Cass

Chapter 11: Your Personal Success Strategy

The best way to discover your strengths, skills, and talents in order to pursue your success is to create and implement your own personal success plan. Everybody is unique, so your plan may be entirely different from the plan of the person next to you. The most important thing to consider when developing your plan is to make sure it is customized to fit *you*. This book has been filled with all sorts of information and you might be feeling a bit overwhelmed at this point. This chapter will serve as a refresher as well as a tool to help you develop a personally customized action plan that will help you put everything you've learned together.

Step 1: Mental Strategies

The best way to strive toward success is to go into it with a sharp, solid state of mind so the first thing you should plan on is figuring out your mental strategies. First, determine if you want to create a morning/evening ritual. I believe having a morning ritual is the most effective although it is beneficial to have both. Doing this can also help you establish good habits, which will come in handy later. Base your ritual off your own schedule, because not everybody's is the same. Grab your journal and write down some ideas on how to develop a morning/evening ritual based off your day-to-day life, your needs, and your priorities.

Second, define and state your goals about success. A good way to start is to define your core values. For many people, their core values are family, health, finances or something along those lines. This is important because your values often serve as your number one motivation. I know many people who are working hard toward success because they want to provide for and take care of their family. Some people work toward success because they want to be financially secure and not have to worry about working hard later in life. Defining your core values is similar to figuring out your "why" for your goals.

Next, set a deadline for your goals. Make the deadline for your short-term goals closer and try to get them to add up to the due date for your long-term goal. Don't forget to be realistic; schedule your goals for a date that is actually physically possible. Hold yourself accountable for your goals by writing in your journal or by brainstorming a few people in your life who can hold you accountable and help you follow up.

Once you've defined your success and stated your goals, begin a daily custom of visualization and positive affirmation. If you've decided to create morning or evening rituals I suggest incorporating these as part of your routine. Brainstorm your five senses and how you can put yourself in the picture of success as powerfully as possible. Now is also a good time to choose some positive affirmations that hit home with you.

Finally, make it a point to mentally prepare yourself for challenges and failures. As hard as you're going to try and avoid them, chances are you will run into an obstacle sooner or later. By mentally preparing yourself for these obstacles now, you stand a much better chance of succeeding.

Step 2: Commit to New Habits and Break Bad Ones

Once you've completed the preparation of your mental strategies, the next step is to commit to as many new good habits as necessary, and start erasing some of your bad habits. On a piece of paper or in your journal, divide a page by drawing a line down the middle. In the right-hand column, write down any good habits that you want to commit to and in the left-hand column, write down any bad habits you currently have but want to erase. For every good habit you successfully pick up, make it a goal to erase one bad habit. Use reminders, exert self-discipline and willpower, or do whatever it takes until you can successfully complete the right column and wipe out the left one.

Step 3: Create Your Diet/Health/Exercise Plan

I've emphasized throughout this book how important your diet and health are; if you've read any of my other books, you're probably familiar with that by now. To ensure that you achieve success quickly and efficiently, part of your plan should be to get yourself in the best possible health. The first step in doing this is to review your current diet and exercise habits. Do you tend to eat more processed foods, or is your diet all natural? How much exercise and physical activity do you get each day? When's the last time you've seen a doctor?

On a piece of paper or in your journal, make a list of foods that you currently eat, then see which of them can be switched out for healthier options. For example, if you eat a lot of white bread, you can easily switch that out for whole wheat or multigrain bread. Do this until you've completely maxed out your options. This can help you start creating a diet plan to ensure that you're only putting the best foods in your body.

Once you've done that, I suggest you analyze your schedule and figure out how you can incorporate exercise. I know not everybody has all the free time in the world so you may need to be creative. If you work sporadic hours, you might find it more convenient just to take walks and exercise at home rather than spend money on a gym membership or a personal trainer. Explore your options and list your resources (YouTube, the internet, home training videos, etc).

Finally, you may want to consider trying out some vitamins, minerals, or supplements. You can use the strategy I use (which I talk about in Chapter 3) or you can experiment on your own. I would recommend talking to your doctor first to make sure that what you decide to try is good for your body.

Step 4: Identify Areas to Improve for Productivity

Once you've established your health plan, the next step is to figure out how you can take advantage of your good health to become more productive. As with many of the steps in this plan, this will depend on your day-to-day schedule. However, the three areas I suggest you focus on for productivity are work, home and your social life. When I say social life, I mean primarily to think about your relationships and figure out which ones are most worth your time. Remember how important it is for success to have strong, supportive, and positive relationships? Make a list of the three most positive relationships you have with people and start spending more time with those people, if you can. Odds are, if you spend time with those friends, they can help you come up with ideas for becoming more productive at work and at home. Think back to all the great habits you discovered that can help your productivity.

Step 5: Practice Self-Confidence Skills

Once you've figured out how you can be more productive in life, get to work on your self-confidence skills; these can only help push you even further! Take a few moments and think about what drags your self-confidence down the most. Is it the way you dress? If so, grab a friend whose style you admire and get him or her to help you redo your wardrobe until you find clothes that you're proud to be seen in. Do your speaking skills need some work? Practice in front of a pet or your mirror until you're confident enough to talk directly to others. Think about your biggest confidence flaw and brainstorm some ideas on how you can directly address it. Before you know it, you'll be facing things you've feared and never believed you can overcome.

Step 6: Flex Your Creativity

After mastering your confidence skills and all the previous principles, I would highly suggest flexing your creativity muscles next. In other words, don't try to "reinvent the wheel." Many successes have come out of people trying new things, experimenting and asking questions like "what if." If Spielberg never said, "What if dinosaurs ruled the earth," we never would have gotten Jurassic Park. If you're having trouble flexing your creativity, experiment with creative hobbies like writing, painting, drawing, etc. or just keep an idea notebook for when inspiration strikes. Don't be afraid to take pride in your ideas; keep pushing until you've found an idea that just might be the world's next big thing.

Step 7: Organize Your Life, Literally

This step will require much more than a pen and paper. For this step, you'll have to take one day of your life and just ORGANIZE! Organize your house, your workspace, your electronics, and anything you can think of. Trust me, the more your environment is organized, the better you will be able to function. Personally, I think cleaning up and organizing feels great and is a great way to regain your focus. If you're not a fan of organizing, promise yourself a nice reward after you've spent the day cleaning up.

Step 8: Create a Finance Plan

Last but not least, I recommend creating a financial plan so your finances can be one less thing that clutters up your mind. I was able to do this by calculating my monthly income and then adding up all my living expenses (rent, car payments, car insurance, cell phone bill, food, gasoline, entertainment, etc). I know a lot of people just avoid doing this because they don't want to see a negative or bad number but it's the only way to really know where your money is going. If you have bad spending habits, open a checking account and use a debit card for all your purchases so you can easily track your money without having a bunch of cash flowing out to we-know-not-where. Here's one good motivator: the more you work toward being successful, the more money you're likely to make; if your budget looks awful now, just follow the steps in this book, work your way toward success and watch your numbers magically reverse! Before you know it, your bank account will start growing as well as your confidence and you'll have more time and energy to focus on being even more successful.

Conclusion

I hope this book was able to help you to discover how to be more successful, how to change your lifestyle to achieve success, and how to bring out the best in yourself.

The next step is to pursue balance in your life.

As I'm sure you've concluded by now, this book has covered many areas of life that include multiple success factors—confidence, money, health, motivation, energy, etc. In the end, it's really all about how you balance the parts of your life, your person and your pursuits. Many people are off-balance; they may have a great business but their finances need work. Or, they may be a health buff but their confidence needs a boost. It all depends on you, but the more balanced you can become, the more successful—and the more happy—you're likely to be. My final suggestion is to seriously get your journal moving along and use it, grow with it. Mark off sections of your journal for different areas that need work or buy a series of journals for each area and start there. Refer back to the different chapters of this book for the best advice in each topic. You can also refer to my separate books for more information and advice on all the topics I've covered here. Keep your journal in a place you frequent daily; this will remind you to update it daily. Once you've mastered an area, move on to another area that needs improvement. Continue to do this until you feel unstoppable!

Finally, if you discovered at least one thing that has helped you or that you think would be beneficial to someone else, be sure to take a few seconds to easily post a quick positive review. As an author, your positive feedback is desperately needed. Your highly valuable five star reviews are like a river of golden joy flowing through a sunny forest of mighty trees and beautiful flowers! *To do your good deed in making the world a better place by helping others with your valuable insight, just leave a nice review.*

My Other Books and Audio Books
www.AcesEbooks.com

Peak Performance Books

Health Books

Be sure to check out my audio books as well!

 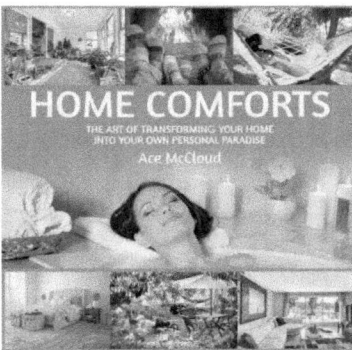 

Check out my website at: **www.AcesEbooks.com** for a complete list of all of my books and high quality audio books. I enjoy bringing you the best knowledge in the world and wish you the best in using this information to make your journey through life better and more enjoyable! **Best of luck to you!**

www.ingramcontent.com/pod-product-compliance
Lightning Source LLC
Chambersburg PA
CBHW051421070526
44584CB00023B/3521